MARVEL 100TH ANNIVERSARY

100TH ANNIVERSARY SPECIAL: FANTASTIC FOUR

WRITER: JEN VAN METER
ARTIST: JOANNA ESTEP
LETTERER: VC'S JOE SABINO
COVER ART: JOANNA ESTEP
EDITOR: EMILY SHAW
SENIOR EDITOR: NICK LOWE

100TH ANNIVERSARY SPECIAL: SPIDER-MAN

WRITER: SEAN RYAN
ARTIST: IN-HYUK LEE
LETTERER: VC'S CLAYTON COWLES
COVER ART: IN-HYUK LEE
EDITOR: JAKE THOMAS
SENIOR EDITOR: NICK LOWE

100TH ANNIVERSARY SPECIAL: X-MEN

WRITER: ROBIN FURTH
ARTIST: JASON MASTERS
COLORISTS: JAMES CAMPBELL & VERONICA GANDINI
LETTERER: VC'S CORY PETIT
COVER ART: JASON LATOUR
EDITOR: XANDER JAROWEY
X-MEN GROUP EDITOR: MIKE MARTS

100TH ANNIVERSARY SPECIAL: AVENGERS

WRITER, ARTIST, LETTERER & COVER ART: JAMES STOKOE
EDITOR: JON MOISAN

100TH ANNIVERSARY SPECIAL: GUARDIANS OF THE GALAXY

WRITERS: ANDY LANNING & RON MARZ
ARTIST: GUSTAVO DUARTE
COLORIST: EDGAR DELGADO
LETTERER: VC'S JOE SABINO
COVER ART: DAVID LOPEZ
EDITOR: DEVIN LEWIS
SENIOR EDITOR: NICK LOWE

COLLECTION EDITOR: MARK D. BEAZLEY
DIGITAL TRAFFIC COORDINATOR: JOE HOCHSTEIN
ASSOCIATE MANAGING EDITOR: ALEX STARBUCK
EDITOR, SPECIAL PROJECTS: JENNIFER GRÜNWALD
SENIOR EDITOR, SPECIAL PROJECTS: JEFF YOUNGQUIST
LAYOUT: JEPH YORK
SVP PRINT, SALES & MARKETING: DAVID GABRIEL
BOOK DESIGN: NELSON RIBEIRO

EDITOR IN CHIEF: AXEL ALONSO
CHIEF CREATIVE OFFICER: JOE QUESADA
PUBLISHER: DAN BUCKLEY
EXECUTIVE PRODUCER: ALAN FINE

MARVEL 100TH ANNIVERSARY. Contains material originally published in magazine form as 100TH ANNIVERSARY SPECIAL: FANTASTIC FOUR #1, 100TH AN...
..., 100TH ANNIVERSARY SPECIAL: AVENGERS #1 and 100TH ANNIVERSARY SPECIAL: GUARDIANS OF THE GALAXY #1. First printing 2014. ISBN# 978-0-7851-5413-6. Published by MARVEL WORLDWIDE, ...
...NTERTAINMENT, LLC. OFFICE OF PUBLICATION: 135 West 50th Street, New York, NY 10020. Copyright © 2014 Marvel Characters, Inc. All rights reserved. All characters featured in this issue and the distinctive names and likenesses
...ereof, and all related indicia are trademarks of Marvel Characters, Inc. No similarity between any of the names, characters, persons, and/or institutions in this magazine with those of any living or dead person or institution is intended,
...nd any such similarity which may exist is purely coincidental. Printed in Canada. ALAN FINE, EVP - Office of the President, Marvel Worldwide, Inc. and EVP & CMO Marvel Characters B.V.; DAN BUCKLEY, Publisher & President - Print,
...nimation & Digital Divisions; JOE QUESADA, Chief Creative Officer; TOM BREVOORT, SVP of Publishing; DAVID BOGART, SVP of Operations & Procurement, Publishing; C.B. CEBULSKI, SVP of Creator & Content Development; DAVID
...ABRIEL, SVP Print, Sales & Marketing; JIM O'KEEFE, VP of Operations & Logistics; DAN CARR, Executive Director of Publishing Technology; SUSAN CRESPI, Editorial Operations Manager; ALEX MORALES, Publishing Operations Manager;
...TAN LEE, Chairman Emeritus. For information regarding advertising in Marvel Comics or on Marvel.com, please contact Niza Disla, Director of Marvel Partnerships, at ndisla@marvel.com. For Marvel subscription inquiries, please call
...0-217-9158. Manufactured between 8/29/2014 and 10/6/2014 by SOLISCO PRINTERS, SCOTT, QC, CANADA.
0987654321

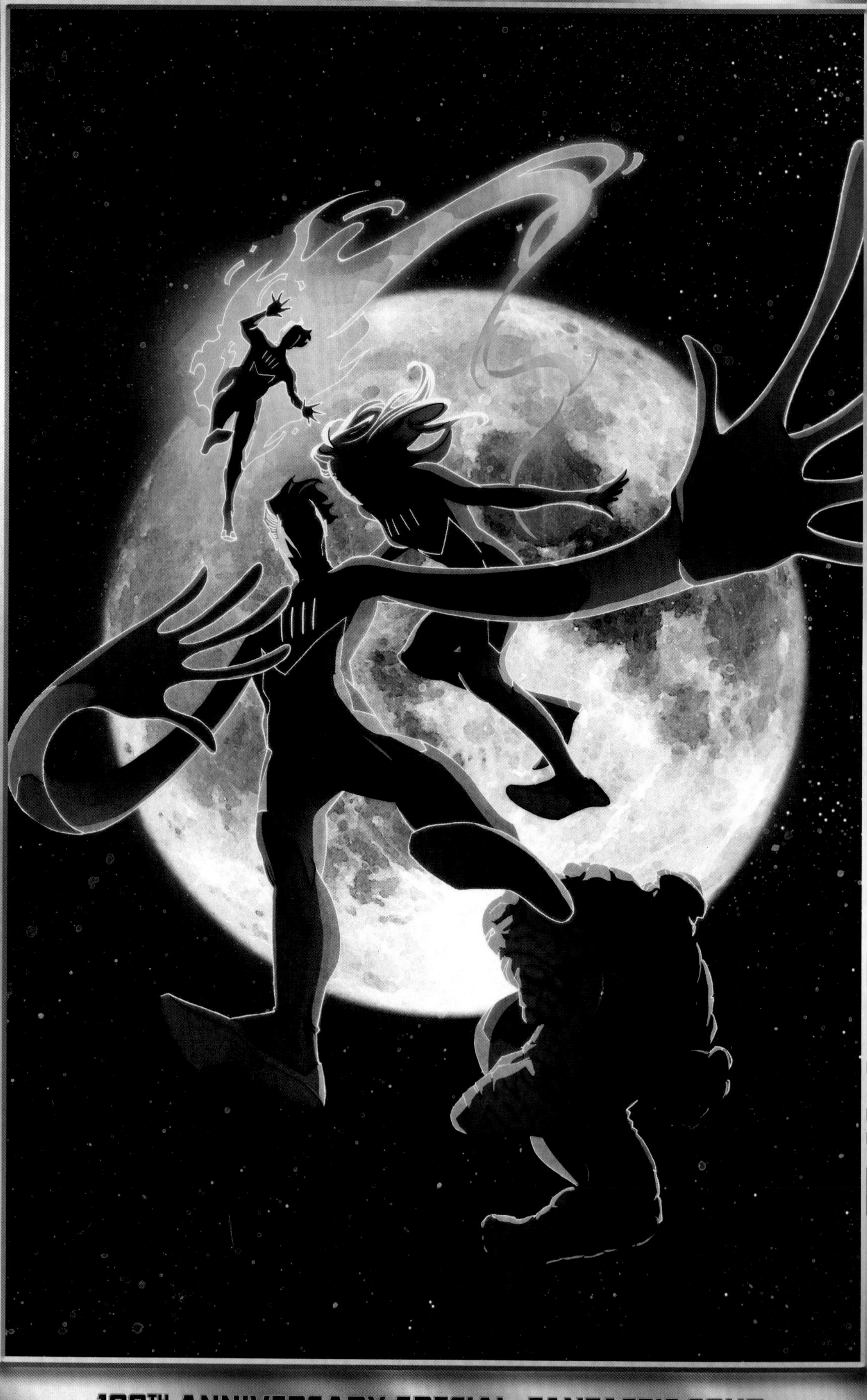

100TH ANNIVERSARY SPECIAL: FANTASTIC FOUR

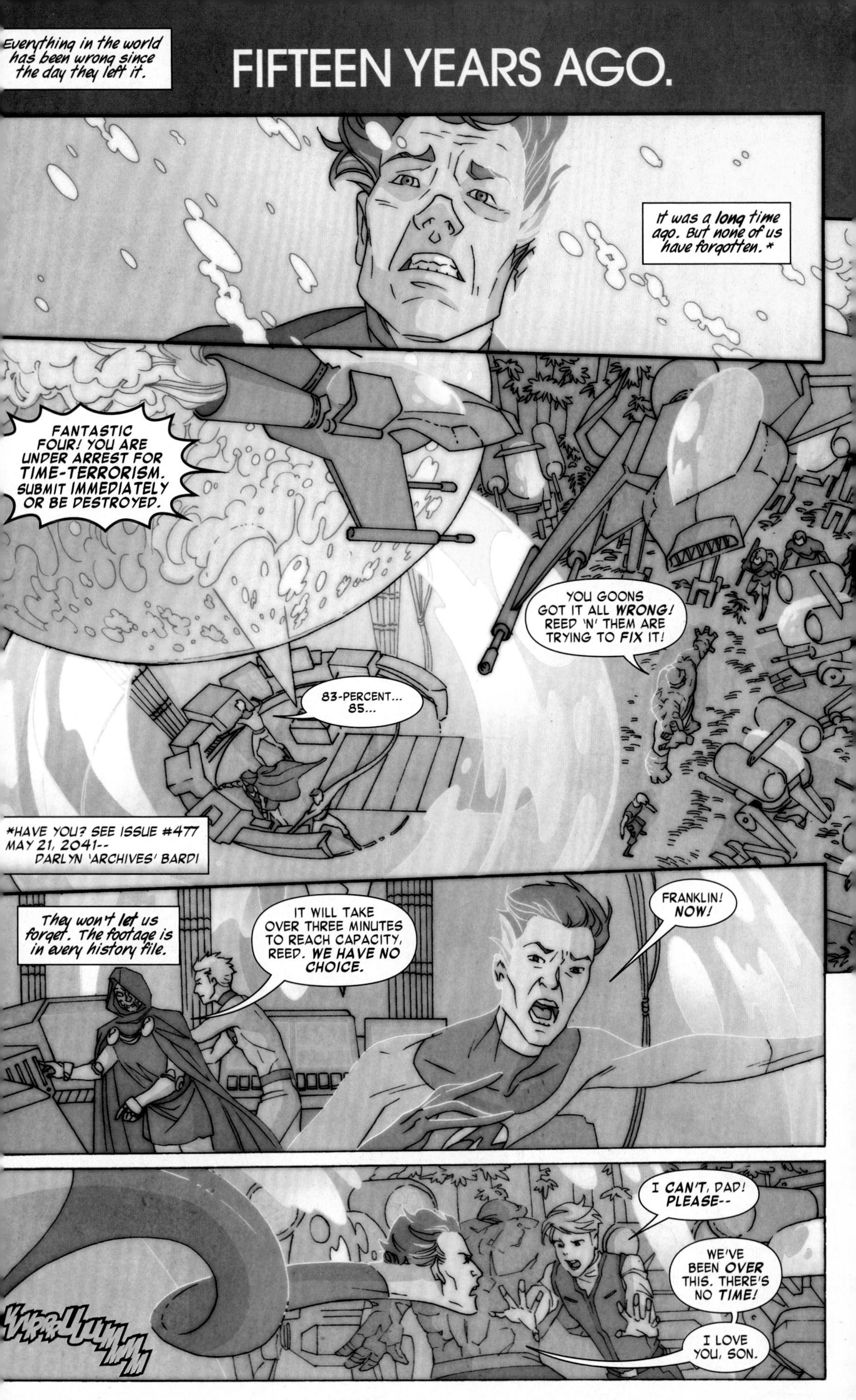
Everything in the world has been wrong since the day they left it.
FIFTEEN YEARS AGO.
It was a long time ago. But none of us have forgotten.*
FANTASTIC FOUR! YOU ARE UNDER ARREST FOR TIME-TERRORISM. SUBMIT IMMEDIATELY OR BE DESTROYED.
YOU GOONS GOT IT ALL WRONG! REED 'N' THEM ARE TRYING TO FIX IT!
83-PERCENT... 85...
*HAVE YOU? SEE ISSUE #477 MAY 21, 2041-- DARLYN 'ARCHIVES' BARDI
They won't let us forget. The footage is in every history file.
IT WILL TAKE OVER THREE MINUTES TO REACH CAPACITY, REED. WE HAVE NO CHOICE.
FRANKLIN! NOW!
I CAN'T, DAD! PLEASE--
WE'VE BEEN OVER THIS. THERE'S NO TIME!
I LOVE YOU, SON.

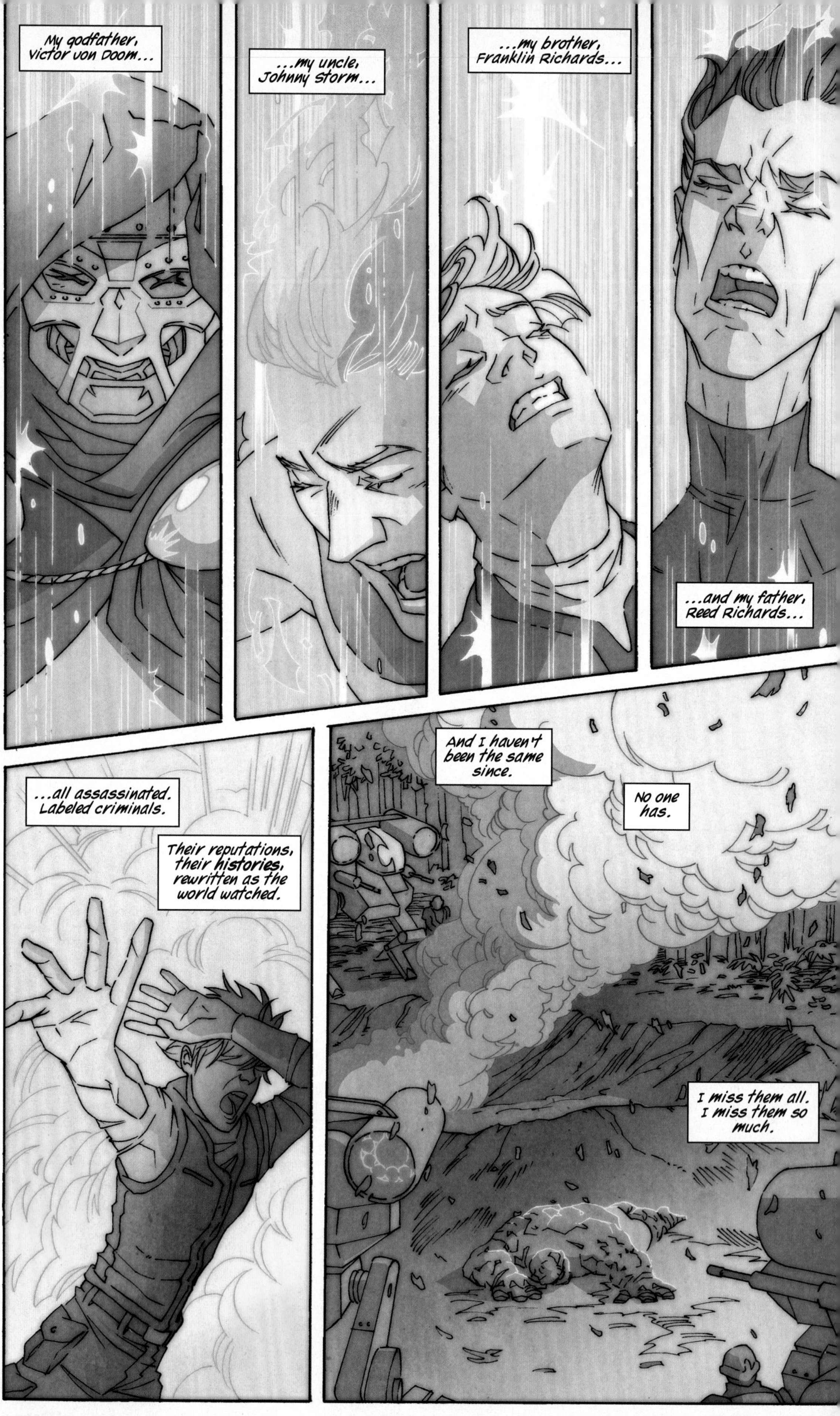
My godfather, Victor von Doom...
...my uncle, Johnny Storm...
...my brother, Franklin Richards...
...and my father, Reed Richards...
...all assassinated. Labeled criminals.
Their reputations, their histories, rewritten as the world watched.
And I haven't been the same since.
No one has.
I miss them all. I miss them so much.

The worlds hate their names.
The worlds need their help.
Soving mysteries, saving the universe--
--they are the

FANTASTIC FOUR

rin Richards-Banner   Kirby Richards-Banner   Victoria Harkness   Lee Minh Cam

Fantasm   Slip   Enchantress   The Human Torch

atastrophic damage to the Neolunar Orbital Colony Perrin! The Fantastic Four were sent to investigate the time-crime scene.

am and Trin confirmed the existence of the previously-theoretical Lunarian Tempusects...the hard way—yeowch!

Meanwhile, Vicky and Kirby are still pretending that kiss didn't happen...

nd Mission Control, Valeria Richards received an alarming 'transmission'! It sounded like...Franklin?

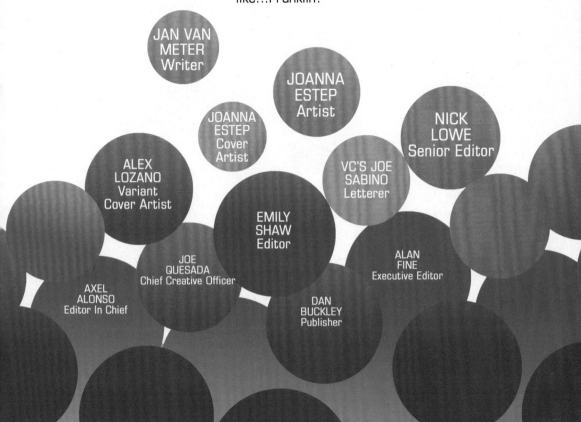

JAN VAN METER
Writer

JOANNA ESTEP
Artist

JOANNA ESTEP
Cover Artist

NICK LOWE
Senior Editor

ALEX LOZANO
Variant Cover Artist

VC'S JOE SABINO
Letterer

EMILY SHAW
Editor

JOE QUESADA
Chief Creative Officer

ALAN FINE
Executive Editor

AXEL ALONSO
Editor In Chief

DAN BUCKLEY
Publisher

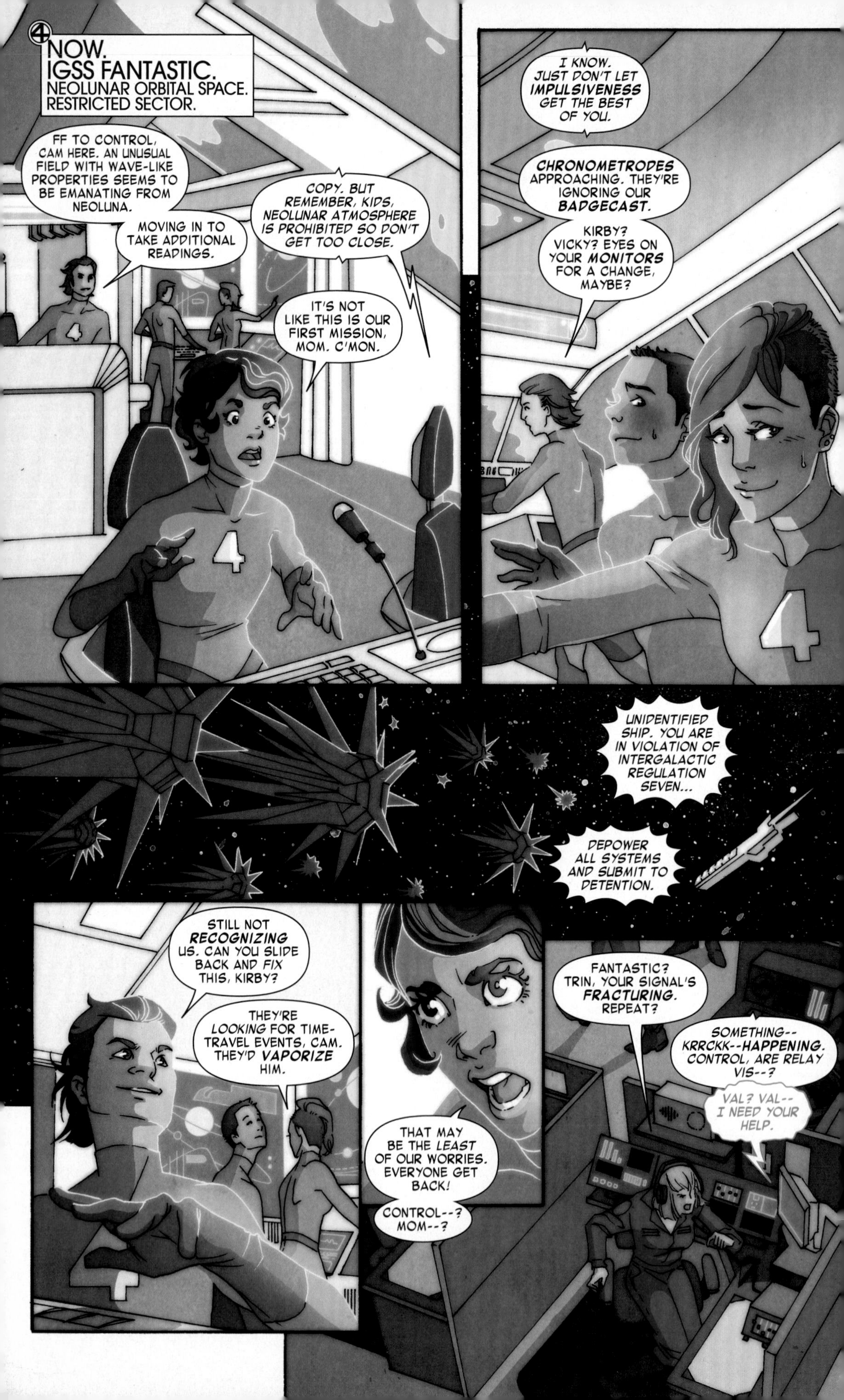

NOW.
IGSS FANTASTIC.
NEOLUNAR ORBITAL SPACE.
RESTRICTED SECTOR.
FF TO CONTROL, CAM HERE. AN UNUSUAL FIELD WITH WAVE-LIKE PROPERTIES SEEMS TO BE EMANATING FROM NEOLUNA.
MOVING IN TO TAKE ADDITIONAL READINGS.
COPY. BUT REMEMBER, KIDS, NEOLUNAR ATMOSPHERE IS PROHIBITED SO DON'T GET TOO CLOSE.
IT'S NOT LIKE THIS IS OUR FIRST MISSION, MOM. C'MON.
I KNOW. JUST DON'T LET IMPULSIVENESS GET THE BEST OF YOU.
CHRONOMETRODES APPROACHING. THEY'RE IGNORING OUR BADGECAST.
KIRBY? VICKY? EYES ON YOUR MONITORS FOR A CHANGE, MAYBE?
UNIDENTIFIED SHIP. YOU ARE IN VIOLATION OF INTERGALACTIC REGULATION SEVEN...
DEPOWER ALL SYSTEMS AND SUBMIT TO DETENTION.
STILL NOT RECOGNIZING US. CAN YOU SLIDE BACK AND FIX THIS, KIRBY?
THEY'RE LOOKING FOR TIME-TRAVEL EVENTS, CAM. THEY'D VAPORIZE HIM.
THAT MAY BE THE LEAST OF OUR WORRIES. EVERYONE GET BACK!
CONTROL--? MOM--?
FANTASTIC? TRIN, YOUR SIGNAL'S FRACTURING. REPEAT?
SOMETHING-- KRRCKK--HAPPENING. CONTROL, ARE RELAY VIS--?
VAL? VAL-- I NEED YOUR HELP.

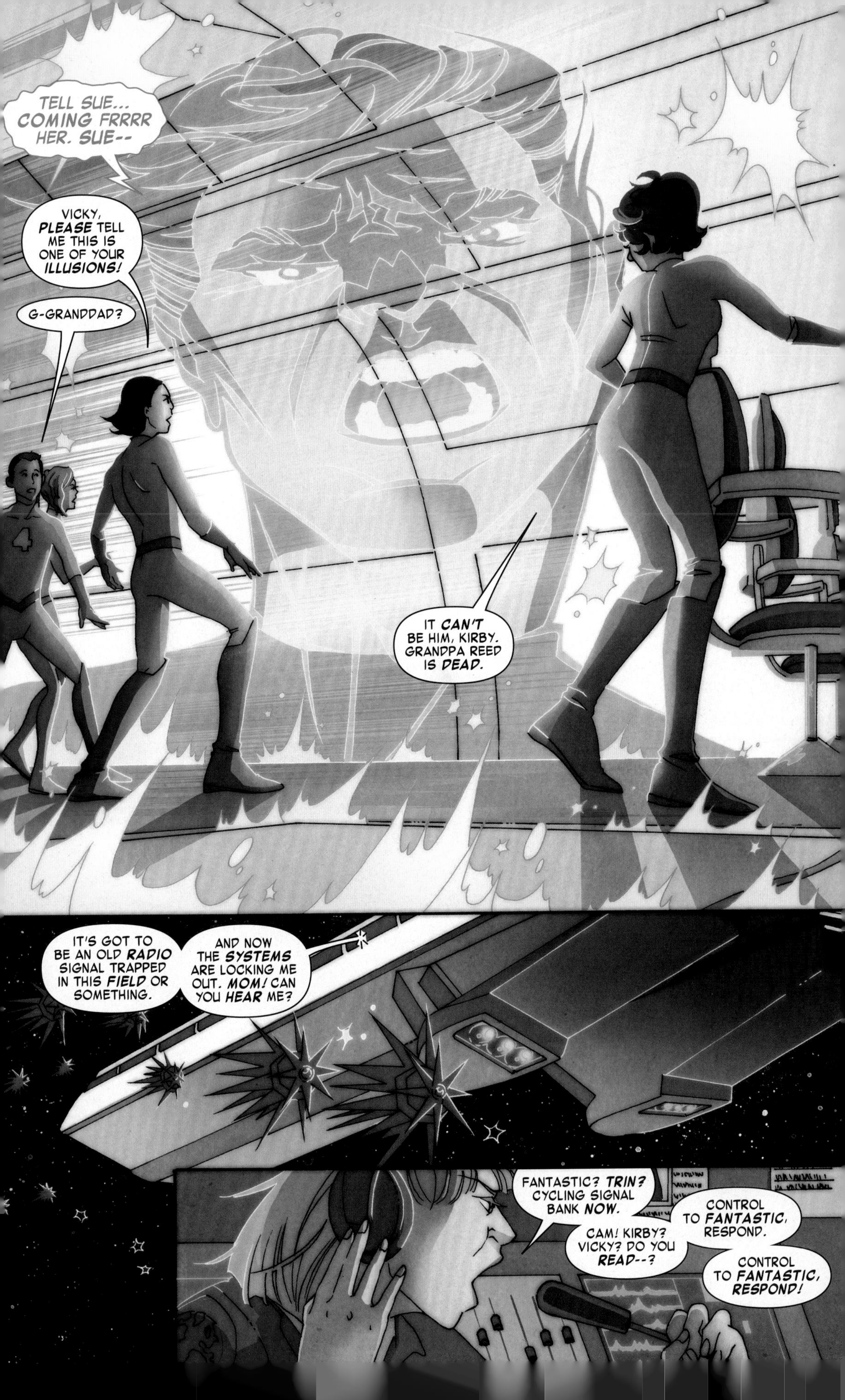
TELL SUE... COMING FRRRR HER. SUE--
VICKY, PLEASE TELL ME THIS IS ONE OF YOUR ILLUSIONS!
G-GRANDDAD?
IT CAN'T BE HIM, KIRBY. GRANDPA REED IS DEAD.
IT'S GOT TO BE AN OLD RADIO SIGNAL TRAPPED IN THIS FIELD OR SOMETHING.
AND NOW THE SYSTEMS ARE LOCKING ME OUT. MOM! CAN YOU HEAR ME?
FANTASTIC? TRIN? CYCLING SIGNAL BANK NOW.
CAM! KIRBY? VICKY? DO YOU READ--?
CONTROL TO FANTASTIC, RESPOND.
CONTROL TO FANTASTIC, RESPOND!

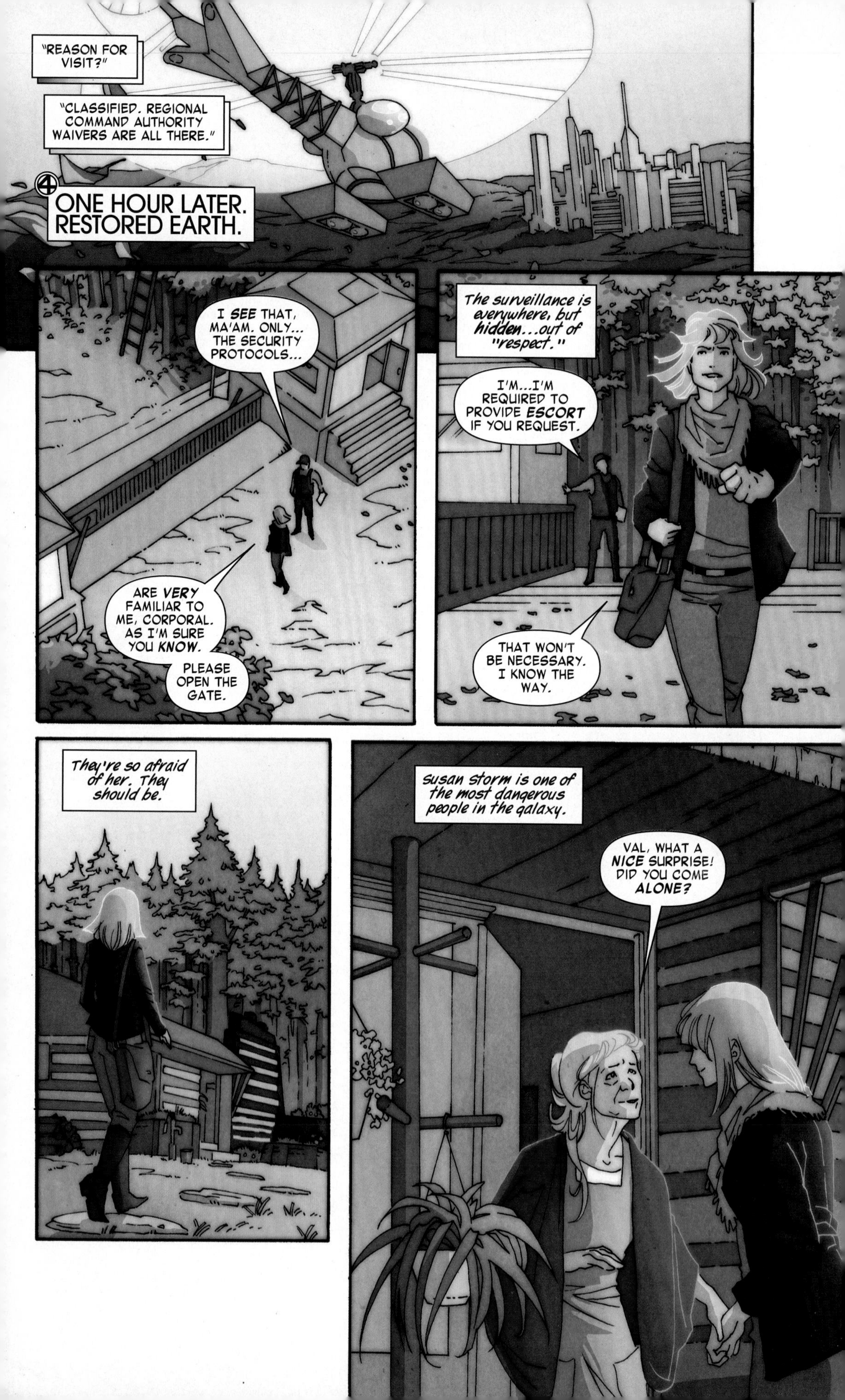
"REASON FOR VISIT?"
"CLASSIFIED. REGIONAL COMMAND AUTHORITY WAIVERS ARE ALL THERE."
ONE HOUR LATER. RESTORED EARTH.
I SEE THAT, MA'AM. ONLY... THE SECURITY PROTOCOLS...
ARE VERY FAMILIAR TO ME, CORPORAL. AS I'M SURE YOU KNOW.
PLEASE OPEN THE GATE.
The surveillance is everywhere, but hidden...out of "respect."
I'M...I'M REQUIRED TO PROVIDE ESCORT IF YOU REQUEST.
THAT WON'T BE NECESSARY. I KNOW THE WAY.
They're so afraid of her. They should be.
Susan Storm is one of the most dangerous people in the galaxy.
VAL, WHAT A NICE SURPRISE! DID YOU COME ALONE?

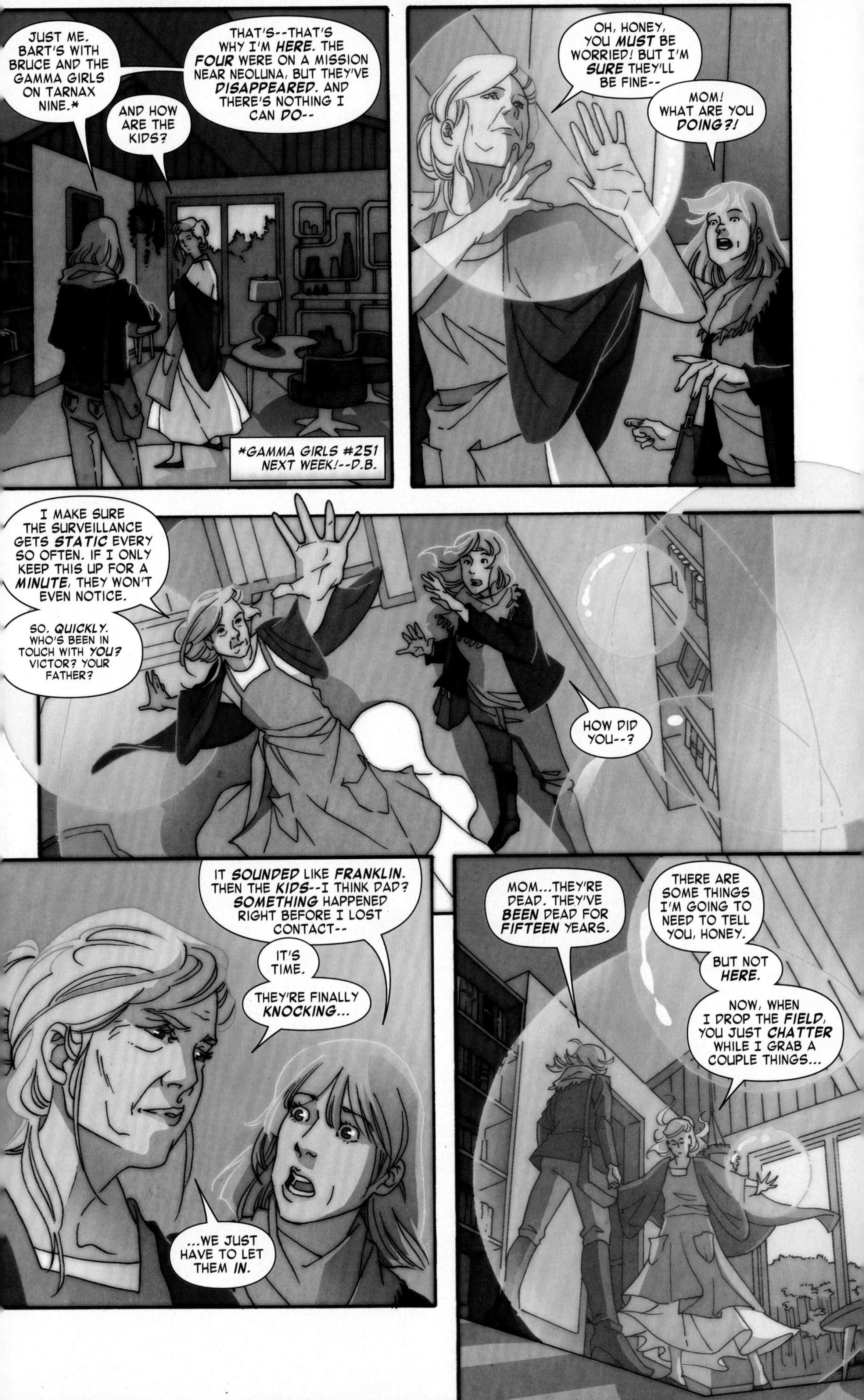

JUST ME. BART'S WITH BRUCE AND THE GAMMA GIRLS ON TARNAX NINE.*
AND HOW ARE THE KIDS?
THAT'S--THAT'S WHY I'M HERE. THE FOUR WERE ON A MISSION NEAR NEOLUNA, BUT THEY'VE DISAPPEARED. AND THERE'S NOTHING I CAN DO--
*GAMMA GIRLS #251 NEXT WEEK!--D.B.
OH, HONEY, YOU MUST BE WORRIED! BUT I'M SURE THEY'LL BE FINE--
MOM! WHAT ARE YOU DOING?!
I MAKE SURE THE SURVEILLANCE GETS STATIC EVERY SO OFTEN. IF I ONLY KEEP THIS UP FOR A MINUTE, THEY WON'T EVEN NOTICE.
SO. QUICKLY. WHO'S BEEN IN TOUCH WITH YOU? VICTOR? YOUR FATHER?
HOW DID YOU--?
IT SOUNDED LIKE FRANKLIN. THEN THE KIDS--I THINK DAD? SOMETHING HAPPENED RIGHT BEFORE I LOST CONTACT--
IT'S TIME.
THEY'RE FINALLY KNOCKING...
...WE JUST HAVE TO LET THEM IN.
MOM...THEY'RE DEAD. THEY'VE BEEN DEAD FOR FIFTEEN YEARS.
THERE ARE SOME THINGS I'M GOING TO NEED TO TELL YOU, HONEY.
BUT NOT HERE.
NOW, WHEN I DROP THE FIELD, YOU JUST CHATTER WHILE I GRAB A COUPLE THINGS...

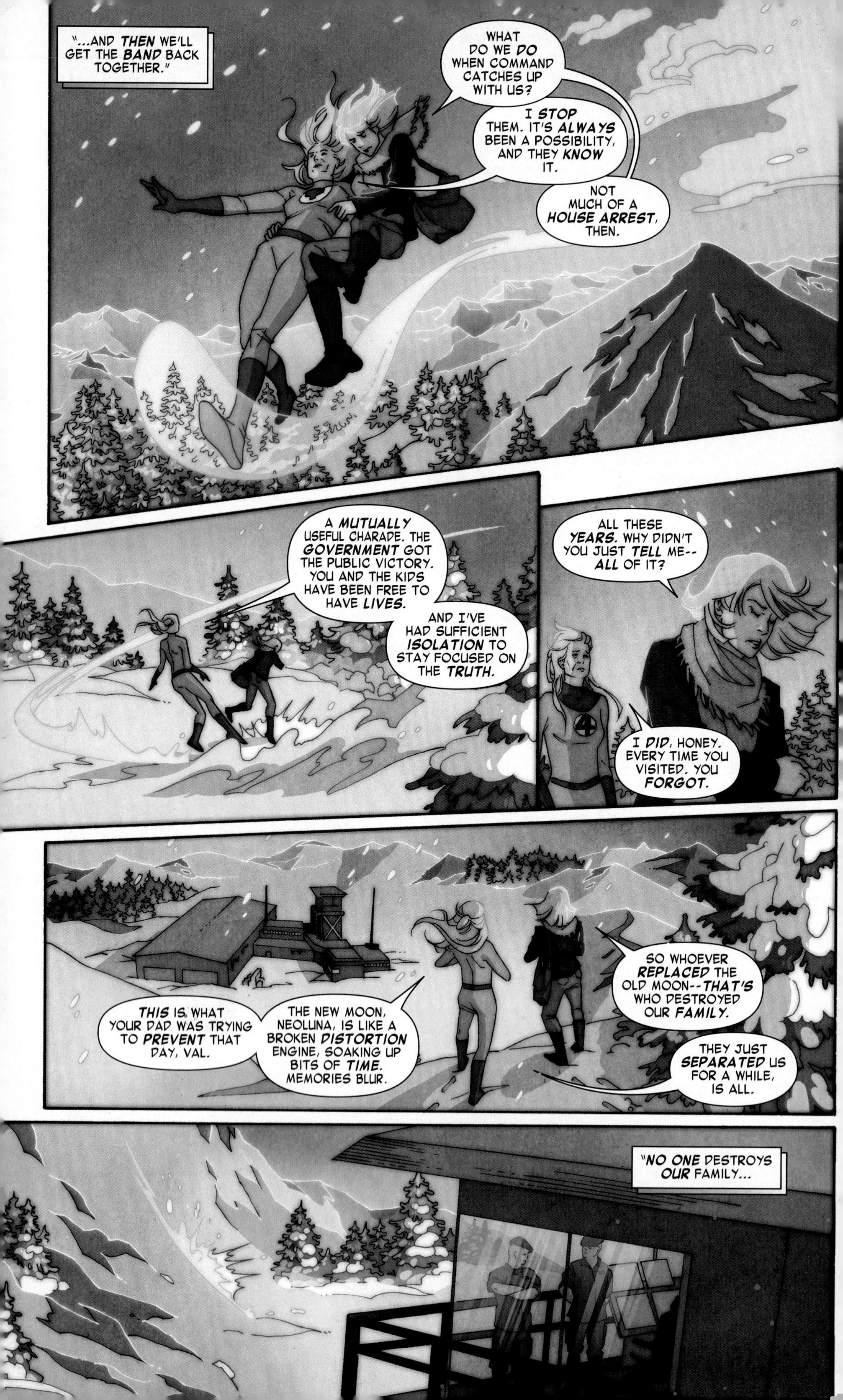
"...AND THEN WE'LL GET THE BAND BACK TOGETHER."
WHAT DO WE DO WHEN COMMAND CATCHES UP WITH US?
I STOP THEM. IT'S ALWAYS BEEN A POSSIBILITY, AND THEY KNOW IT.
NOT MUCH OF A HOUSE ARREST, THEN.
A MUTUALLY USEFUL CHARADE. THE GOVERNMENT GOT THE PUBLIC VICTORY. YOU AND THE KIDS HAVE BEEN FREE TO HAVE LIVES.
AND I'VE HAD SUFFICIENT ISOLATION TO STAY FOCUSED ON THE TRUTH.
ALL THESE YEARS. WHY DIDN'T YOU JUST TELL ME-- ALL OF IT?
I DID, HONEY. EVERY TIME YOU VISITED. YOU FORGOT.
THIS IS WHAT YOUR DAD WAS TRYING TO PREVENT THAT DAY, VAL.
THE NEW MOON, NEOLUNA, IS LIKE A BROKEN DISTORTION ENGINE, SOAKING UP BITS OF TIME. MEMORIES BLUR.
SO WHOEVER REPLACED THE OLD MOON--THAT'S WHO DESTROYED OUR FAMILY.
THEY JUST SEPARATED US FOR A WHILE, IS ALL.
"NO ONE DESTROYS OUR FAMILY...

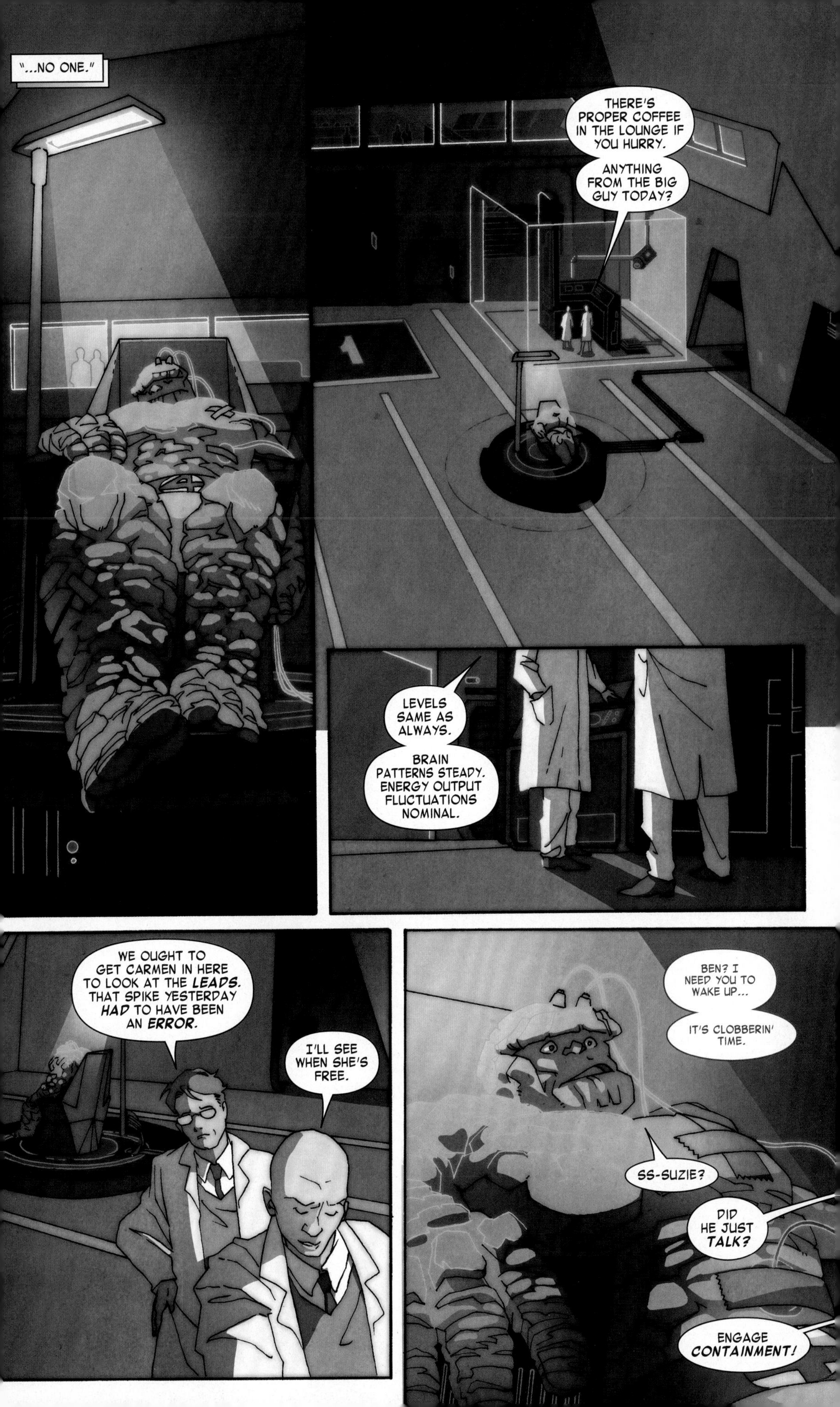
"...NO ONE."
THERE'S PROPER COFFEE IN THE LOUNGE IF YOU HURRY.
ANYTHING FROM THE BIG GUY TODAY?
LEVELS SAME AS ALWAYS.
BRAIN PATTERNS STEADY. ENERGY OUTPUT FLUCTUATIONS NOMINAL.
WE OUGHT TO GET CARMEN IN HERE TO LOOK AT THE LEADS. THAT SPIKE YESTERDAY HAD TO HAVE BEEN AN ERROR.
I'LL SEE WHEN SHE'S FREE.
BEN? I NEED YOU TO WAKE UP...
IT'S CLOBBERIN' TIME.
SS-SUZIE?
DID HE JUST TALK?
ENGAGE CONTAINMENT!

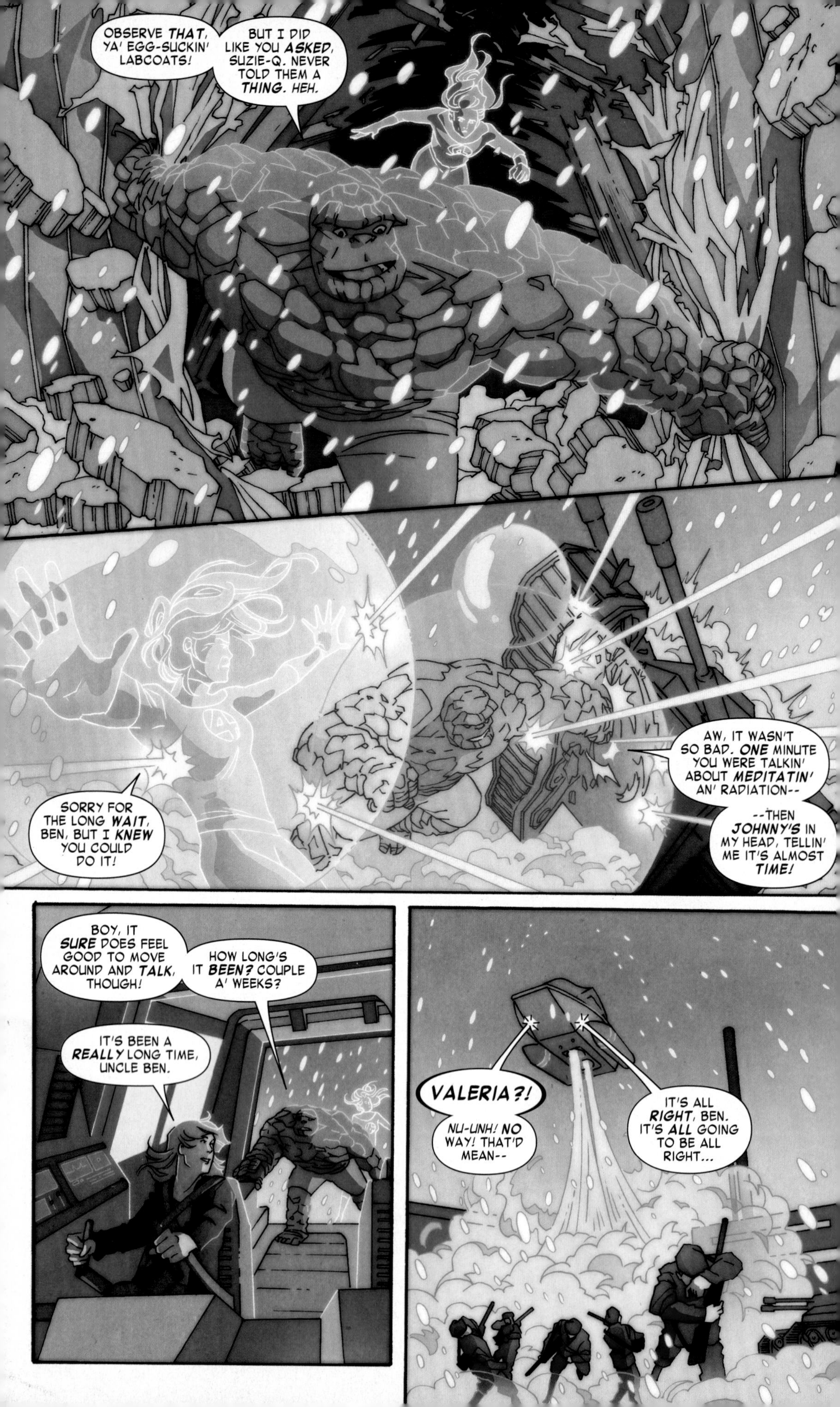

OBSERVE THAT, YA' EGG-SUCKIN' LABCOATS!
BUT I DID LIKE YOU ASKED, SUZIE-Q. NEVER TOLD THEM A THING. HEH.
SORRY FOR THE LONG WAIT, BEN, BUT I KNEW YOU COULD DO IT!
AW, IT WASN'T SO BAD. ONE MINUTE YOU WERE TALKIN' ABOUT MEDITATIN' AN' RADIATION--
--THEN JOHNNY'S IN MY HEAD, TELLIN' ME IT'S ALMOST TIME!
BOY, IT SURE DOES FEEL GOOD TO MOVE AROUND AND TALK, THOUGH!
HOW LONG'S IT BEEN? COUPLE A' WEEKS?
IT'S BEEN A REALLY LONG TIME, UNCLE BEN.
VALERIA?!
NU-UNH! NO WAY! THAT'D MEAN--
IT'S ALL RIGHT, BEN. IT'S ALL GOING TO BE ALL RIGHT...

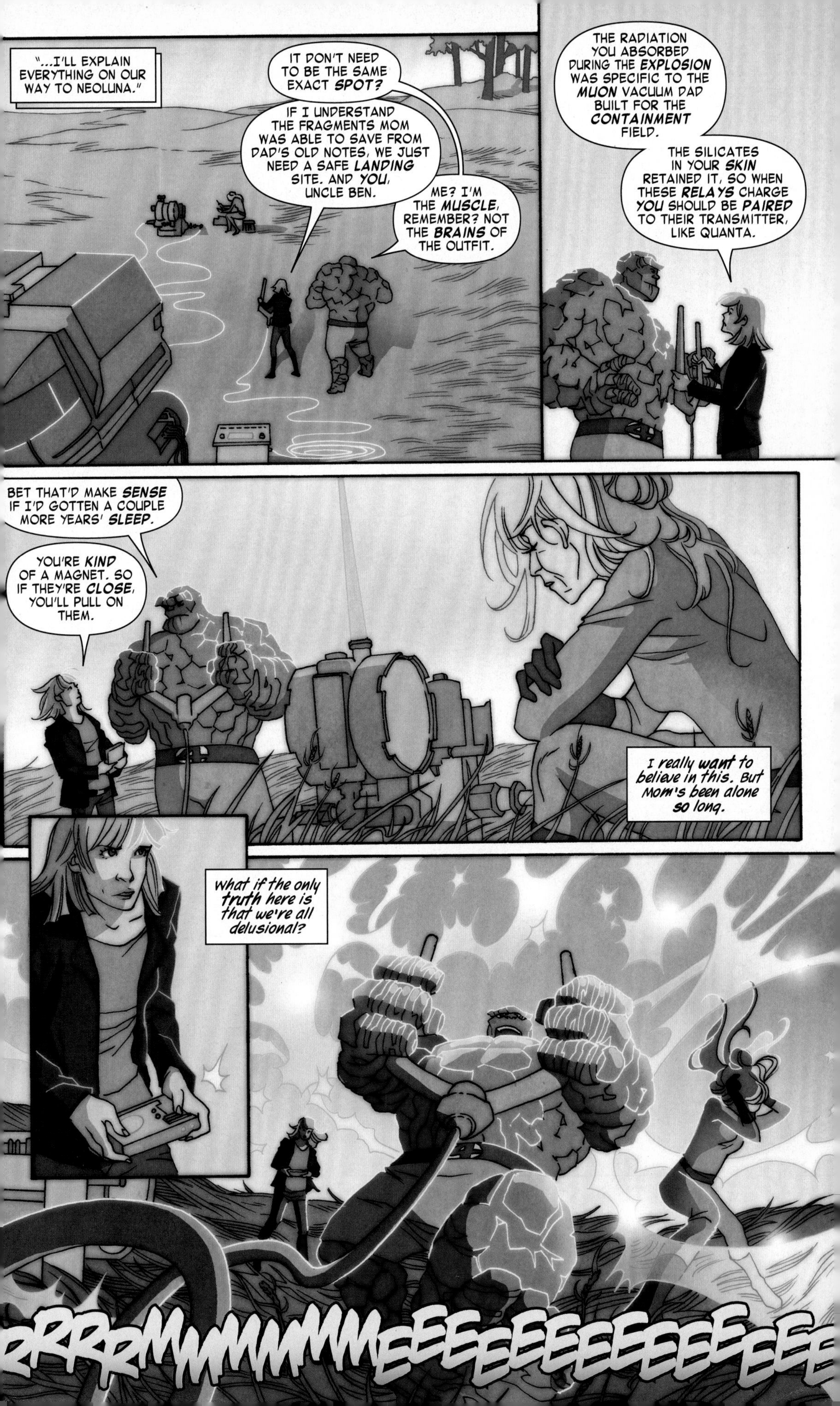

"...I'LL EXPLAIN EVERYTHING ON OUR WAY TO NEOLUNA."
IT DON'T NEED TO BE THE SAME EXACT SPOT?
IF I UNDERSTAND THE FRAGMENTS MOM WAS ABLE TO SAVE FROM DAD'S OLD NOTES, WE JUST NEED A SAFE LANDING SITE. AND YOU, UNCLE BEN.
ME? I'M THE MUSCLE, REMEMBER? NOT THE BRAINS OF THE OUTFIT.
THE RADIATION YOU ABSORBED DURING THE EXPLOSION WAS SPECIFIC TO THE MUON VACUUM DAD BUILT FOR THE CONTAINMENT FIELD.
THE SILICATES IN YOUR SKIN RETAINED IT, SO WHEN THESE RELAYS CHARGE YOU SHOULD BE PAIRED TO THEIR TRANSMITTER, LIKE QUANTA.
BET THAT'D MAKE SENSE IF I'D GOTTEN A COUPLE MORE YEARS' SLEEP.
YOU'RE KIND OF A MAGNET. SO IF THEY'RE CLOSE, YOU'LL PULL ON THEM.
I really want to believe in this. But Mom's been alone so long.
What if the only truth here is that we're all delusional?
RRRRMMMMMMEEEEEEEEEEEEEEE

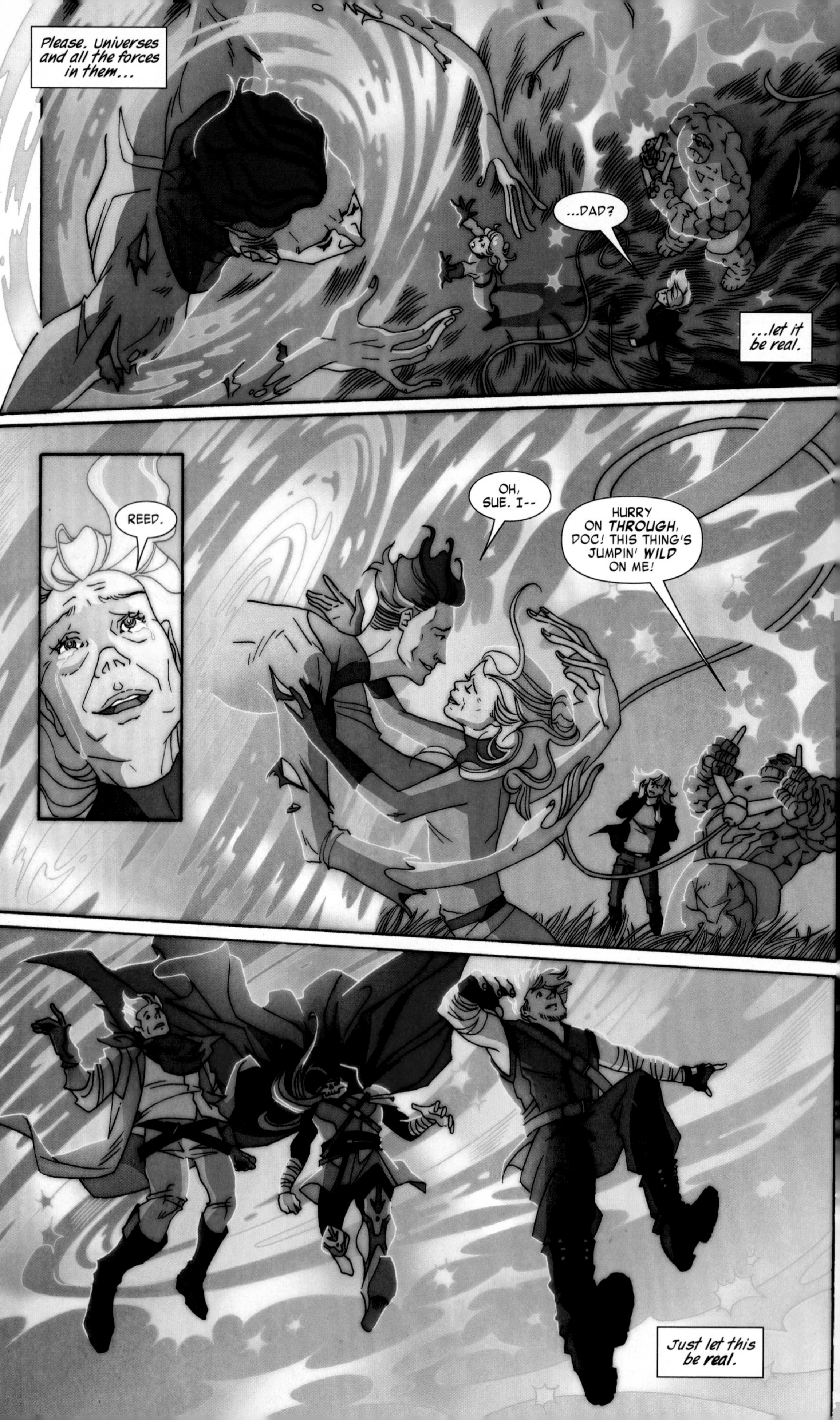
Please. Universes and all the forces in them...
...DAD?
...let it be real.
REED.
OH, SUE. I--
HURRY ON THROUGH, DOC! THIS THING'S JUMPIN' WILD ON ME!
Just let this be real.

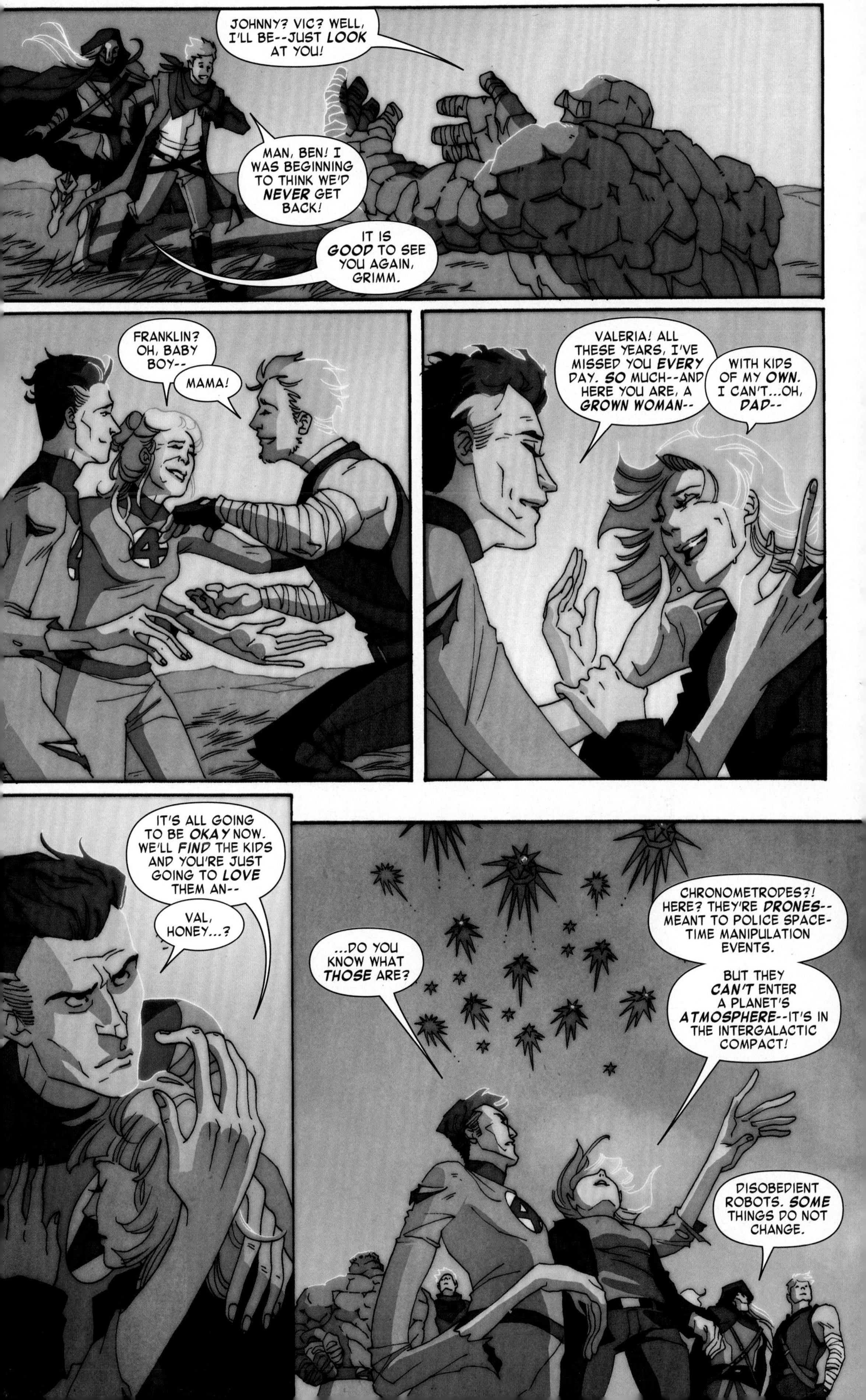
JOHNNY? VIC? WELL, I'LL BE--JUST LOOK AT YOU!
MAN, BEN! I WAS BEGINNING TO THINK WE'D NEVER GET BACK!
IT IS GOOD TO SEE YOU AGAIN, GRIMM.
FRANKLIN? OH, BABY BOY--
MAMA!
VALERIA! ALL THESE YEARS, I'VE MISSED YOU EVERY DAY. SO MUCH--AND HERE YOU ARE, A GROWN WOMAN--
WITH KIDS OF MY OWN. I CAN'T...OH, DAD--
IT'S ALL GOING TO BE OKAY NOW. WE'LL FIND THE KIDS AND YOU'RE JUST GOING TO LOVE THEM AN--
VAL, HONEY...?
...DO YOU KNOW WHAT THOSE ARE?
CHRONOMETRODES?! HERE? THEY'RE DRONES--MEANT TO POLICE SPACE-TIME MANIPULATION EVENTS.
BUT THEY CAN'T ENTER A PLANET'S ATMOSPHERE--IT'S IN THE INTERGALACTIC COMPACT!
DISOBEDIENT ROBOTS. SOME THINGS DO NOT CHANGE.

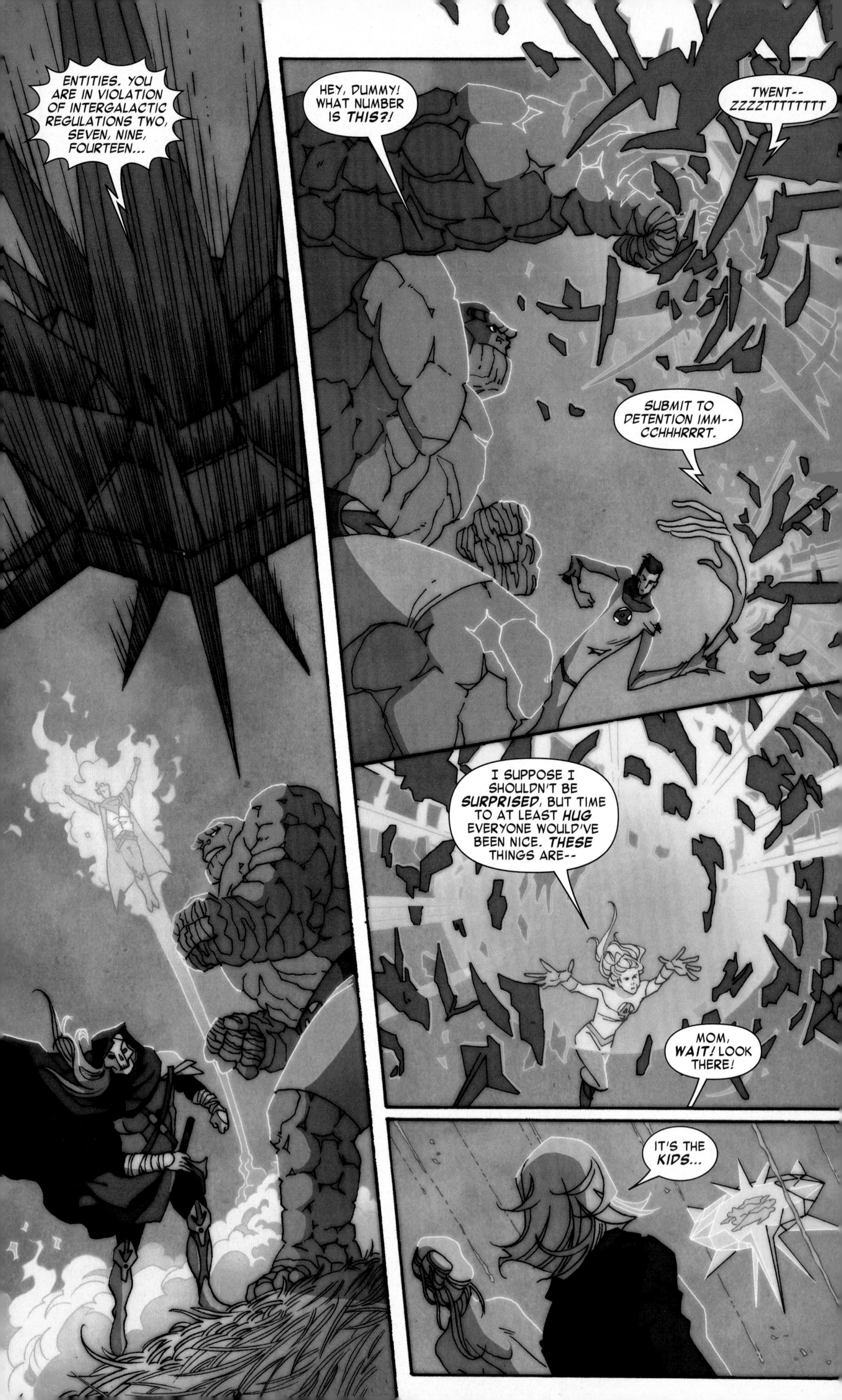
ENTITIES. YOU ARE IN VIOLATION OF INTERGALACTIC REGULATIONS TWO, SEVEN, NINE, FOURTEEN...
HEY, DUMMY! WHAT NUMBER IS THIS?!
TWENT-- ZZZZTTTTTTTTT
SUBMIT TO DETENTION IMM-- CCHHHRRRT.
I SUPPOSE I SHOULDN'T BE SURPRISED, BUT TIME TO AT LEAST HUG EVERYONE WOULD'VE BEEN NICE. THESE THINGS ARE--
MOM, WAIT! LOOK THERE!
IT'S THE KIDS...

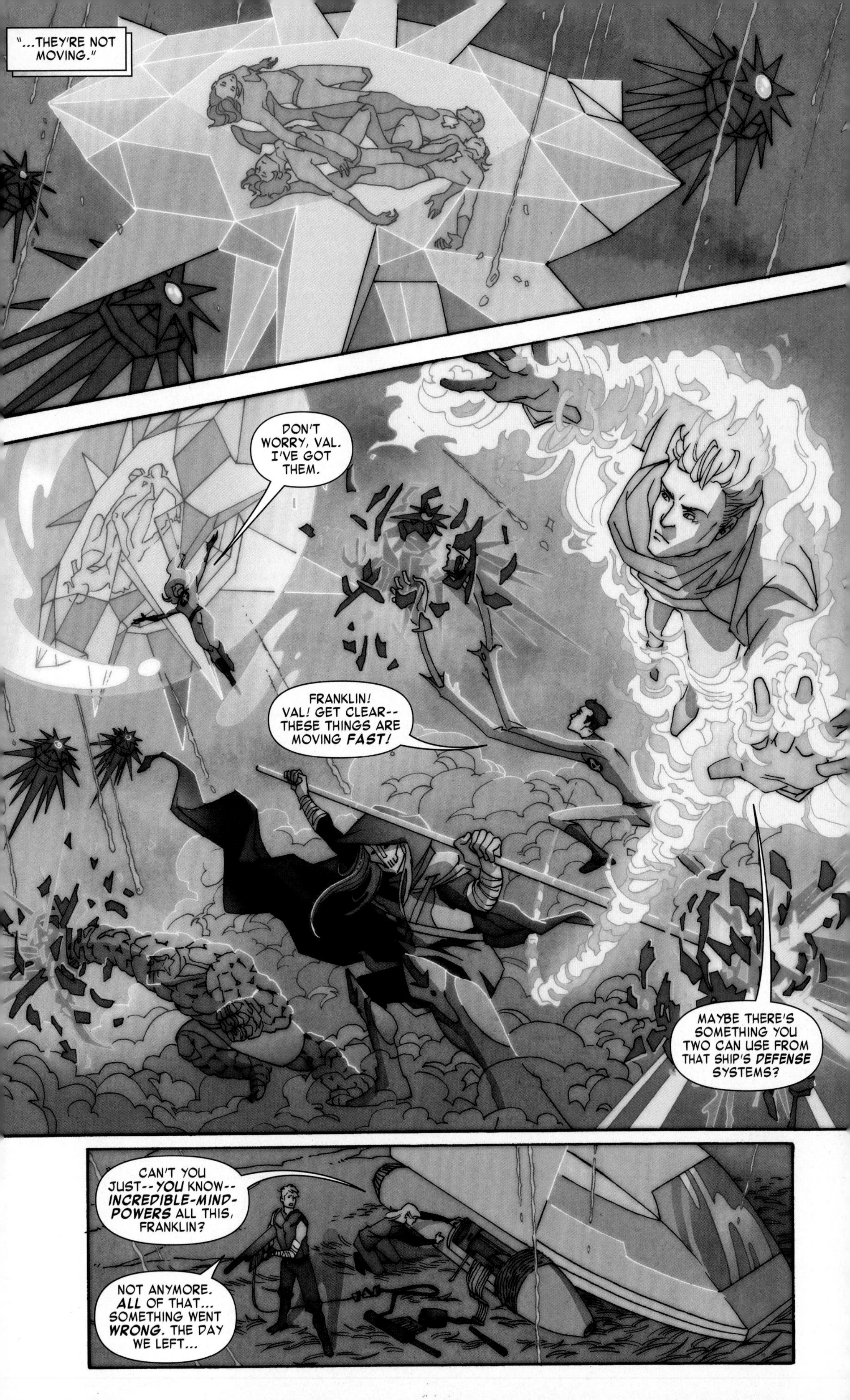
"...THEY'RE NOT MOVING."
DON'T WORRY, VAL. I'VE GOT THEM.
FRANKLIN! VAL! GET CLEAR-- THESE THINGS ARE MOVING *FAST*!
MAYBE THERE'S SOMETHING YOU TWO CAN USE FROM THAT SHIP'S *DEFENSE* SYSTEMS?
CAN'T YOU JUST--*YOU* KNOW--*INCREDIBLE-MIND-POWERS* ALL THIS, FRANKLIN?
NOT ANYMORE. *ALL* OF THAT... SOMETHING WENT *WRONG*. THE DAY WE LEFT...

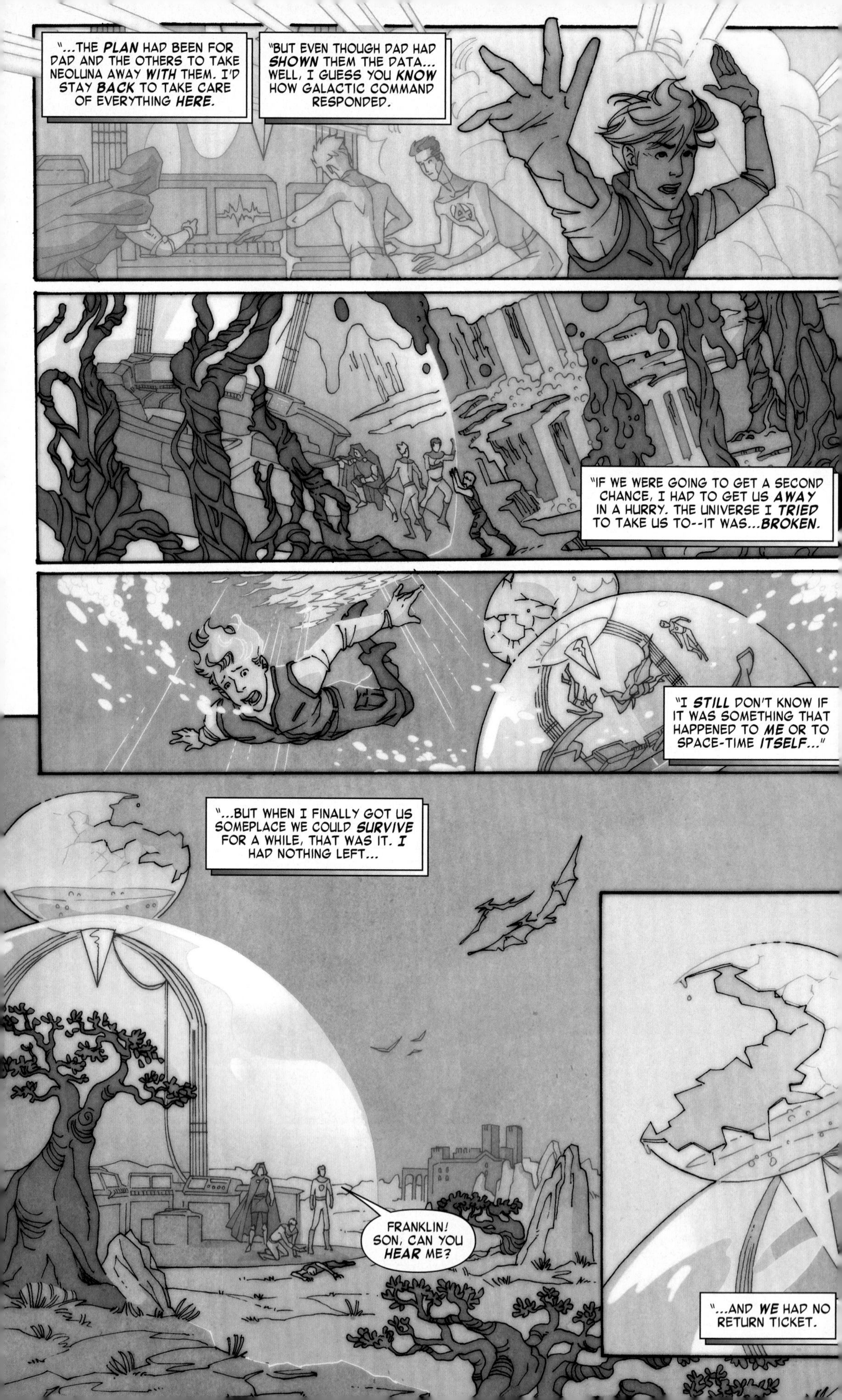
"...THE PLAN HAD BEEN FOR DAD AND THE OTHERS TO TAKE NEOLUNA AWAY WITH THEM. I'D STAY BACK TO TAKE CARE OF EVERYTHING HERE.
"BUT EVEN THOUGH DAD HAD SHOWN THEM THE DATA... WELL, I GUESS YOU KNOW HOW GALACTIC COMMAND RESPONDED.
"IF WE WERE GOING TO GET A SECOND CHANCE, I HAD TO GET US AWAY IN A HURRY. THE UNIVERSE I TRIED TO TAKE US TO--IT WAS...BROKEN.
"I STILL DON'T KNOW IF IT WAS SOMETHING THAT HAPPENED TO ME OR TO SPACE-TIME ITSELF..."
"...BUT WHEN I FINALLY GOT US SOMEPLACE WE COULD SURVIVE FOR A WHILE, THAT WAS IT. I HAD NOTHING LEFT...
FRANKLIN! SON, CAN YOU HEAR ME?
"...AND WE HAD NO RETURN TICKET.

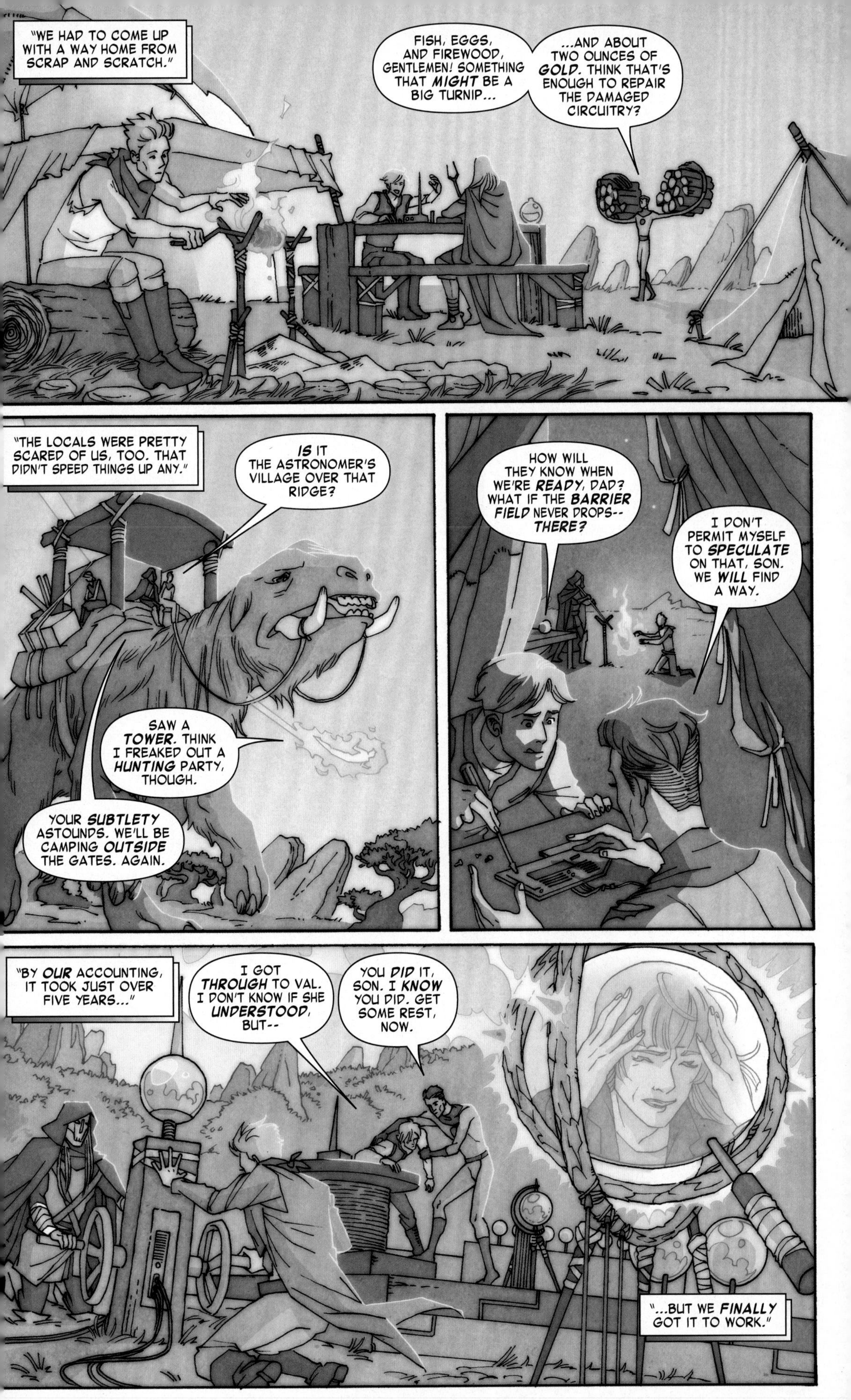
"WE HAD TO COME UP WITH A WAY HOME FROM SCRAP AND SCRATCH."
FISH, EGGS, AND FIREWOOD, GENTLEMEN! SOMETHING THAT MIGHT BE A BIG TURNIP...
...AND ABOUT TWO OUNCES OF GOLD. THINK THAT'S ENOUGH TO REPAIR THE DAMAGED CIRCUITRY?
"THE LOCALS WERE PRETTY SCARED OF US, TOO. THAT DIDN'T SPEED THINGS UP ANY."
IS IT THE ASTRONOMER'S VILLAGE OVER THAT RIDGE?
SAW A TOWER. THINK I FREAKED OUT A HUNTING PARTY, THOUGH.
YOUR SUBTLETY ASTOUNDS. WE'LL BE CAMPING OUTSIDE THE GATES. AGAIN.
HOW WILL THEY KNOW WHEN WE'RE READY, DAD? WHAT IF THE BARRIER FIELD NEVER DROPS-- THERE?
I DON'T PERMIT MYSELF TO SPECULATE ON THAT, SON. WE WILL FIND A WAY.
"BY OUR ACCOUNTING, IT TOOK JUST OVER FIVE YEARS..."
I GOT THROUGH TO VAL. I DON'T KNOW IF SHE UNDERSTOOD, BUT--
YOU DID IT, SON. I KNOW YOU DID. GET SOME REST, NOW.
"...BUT WE FINALLY GOT IT TO WORK."

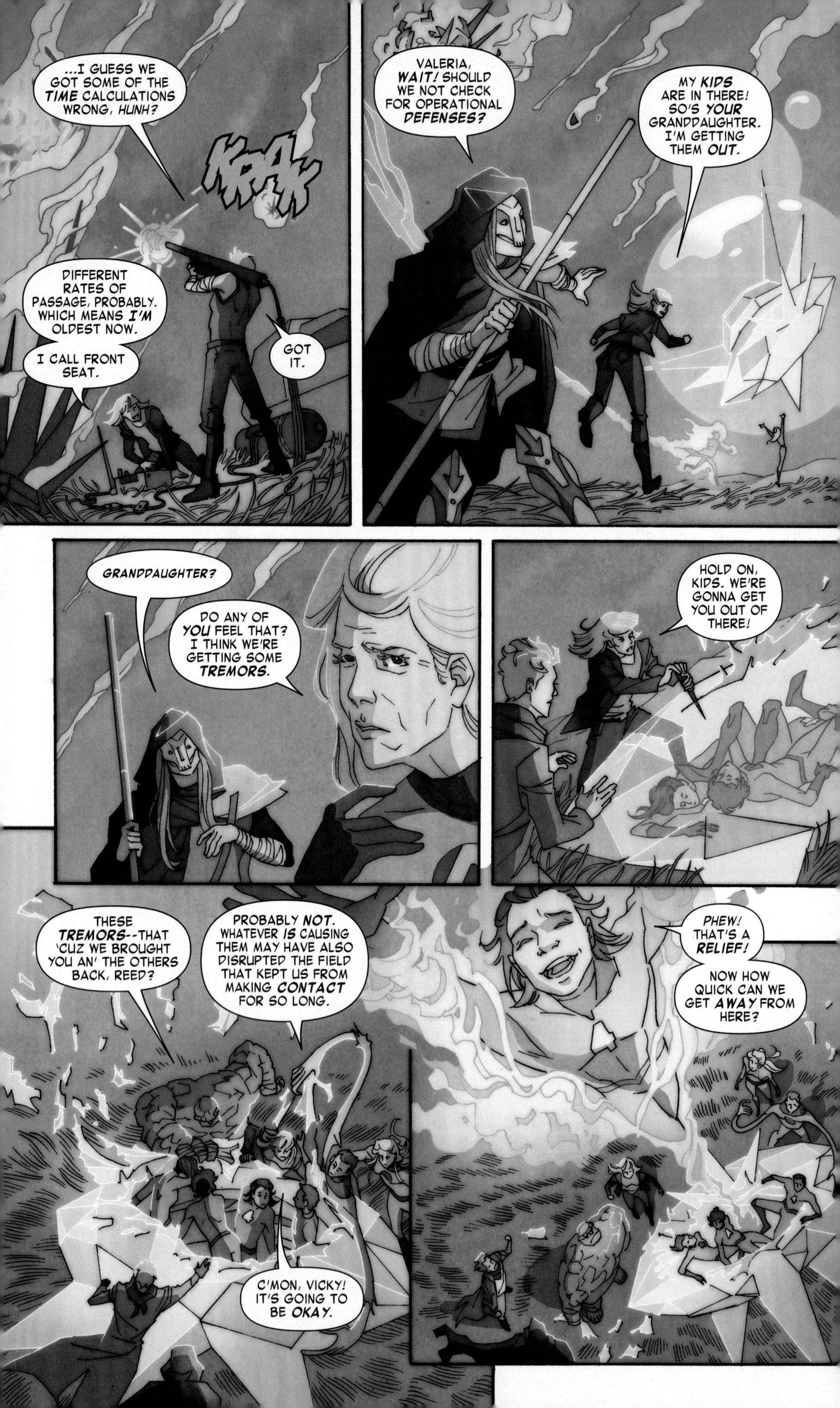

...I GUESS WE GOT SOME OF THE TIME CALCULATIONS WRONG, HUNH?
KRAK
DIFFERENT RATES OF PASSAGE, PROBABLY. WHICH MEANS I'M OLDEST NOW.
I CALL FRONT SEAT.
GOT IT.
VALERIA, WAIT! SHOULD WE NOT CHECK FOR OPERATIONAL DEFENSES?
MY KIDS ARE IN THERE! SO'S YOUR GRANDDAUGHTER. I'M GETTING THEM OUT.
GRANDDAUGHTER?
DO ANY OF YOU FEEL THAT? I THINK WE'RE GETTING SOME TREMORS.
HOLD ON, KIDS. WE'RE GONNA GET YOU OUT OF THERE!
THESE TREMORS--THAT 'CUZ WE BROUGHT YOU AN' THE OTHERS BACK, REED?
PROBABLY NOT. WHATEVER IS CAUSING THEM MAY HAVE ALSO DISRUPTED THE FIELD THAT KEPT US FROM MAKING CONTACT FOR SO LONG.
PHEW! THAT'S A RELIEF!
NOW HOW QUICK CAN WE GET AWAY FROM HERE?
C'MON, VICKY! IT'S GOING TO BE OKAY.

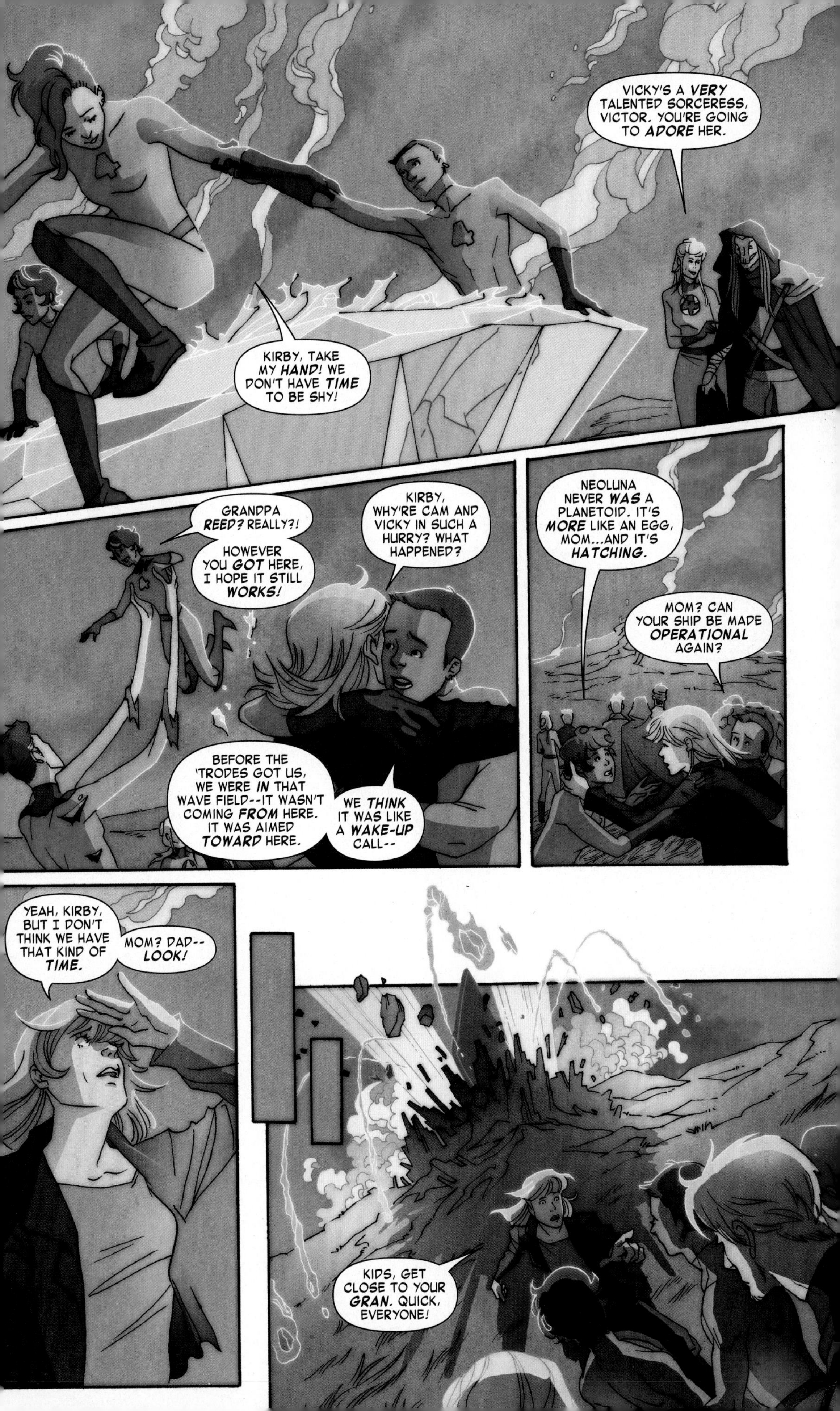
VICKY'S A VERY TALENTED SORCERESS, VICTOR. YOU'RE GOING TO ADORE HER.
KIRBY, TAKE MY HAND! WE DON'T HAVE TIME TO BE SHY!
GRANDPA REED? REALLY?!
HOWEVER YOU GOT HERE, I HOPE IT STILL WORKS!
KIRBY, WHY'RE CAM AND VICKY IN SUCH A HURRY? WHAT HAPPENED?
BEFORE THE 'TRODES GOT US, WE WERE IN THAT WAVE FIELD--IT WASN'T COMING FROM HERE. IT WAS AIMED TOWARD HERE.
WE THINK IT WAS LIKE A WAKE-UP CALL--
NEOLUNA NEVER WAS A PLANETOID. IT'S MORE LIKE AN EGG, MOM...AND IT'S HATCHING.
MOM? CAN YOUR SHIP BE MADE OPERATIONAL AGAIN?
YEAH, KIRBY, BUT I DON'T THINK WE HAVE THAT KIND OF TIME.
MOM? DAD--LOOK!
KIDS, GET CLOSE TO YOUR GRAN. QUICK, EVERYONE!

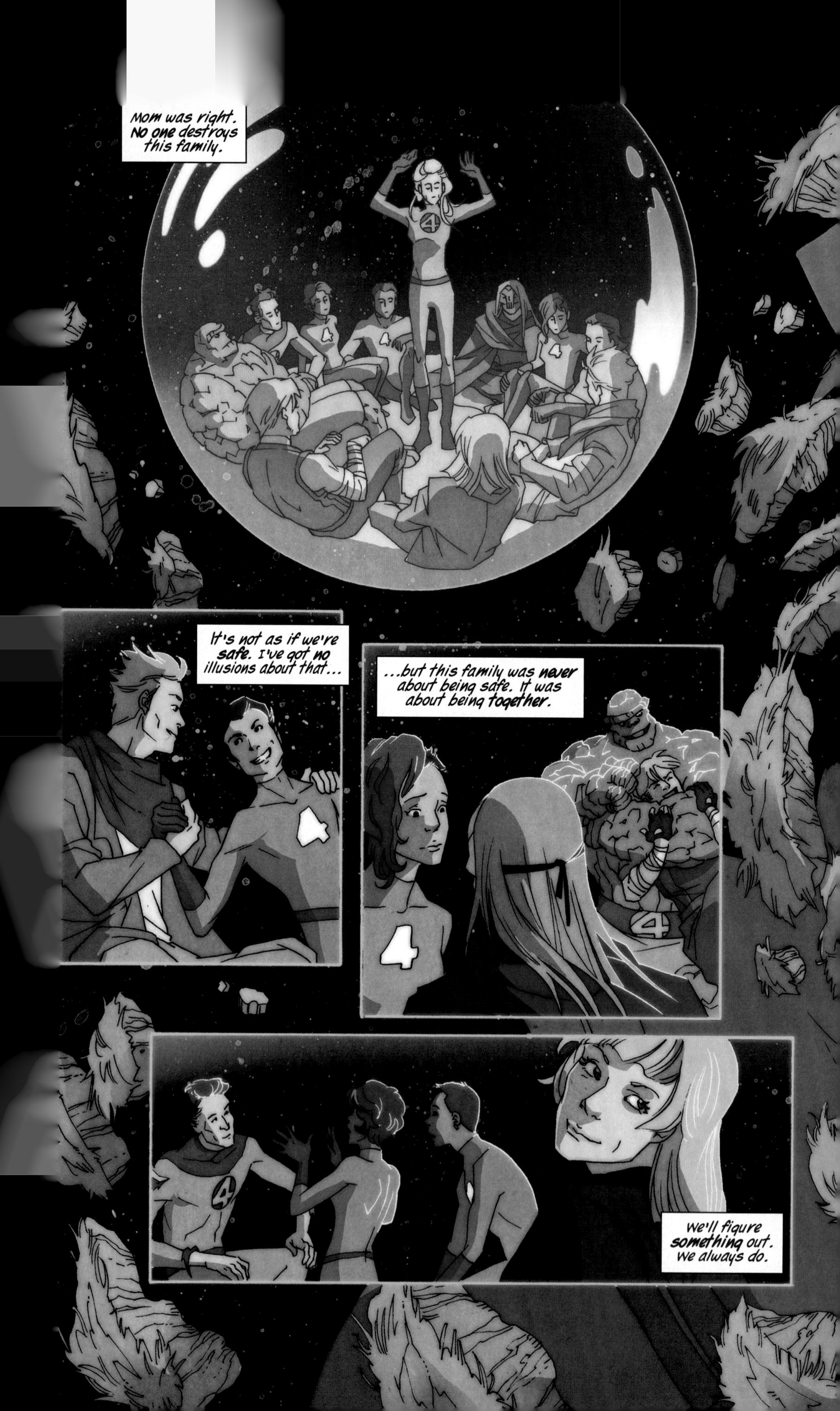
Mom was right. No one destroys this family.
It's not as if we're safe. I've got no illusions about that...
...but this family was never about being safe. It was about being together.
We'll figure something out. We always do.

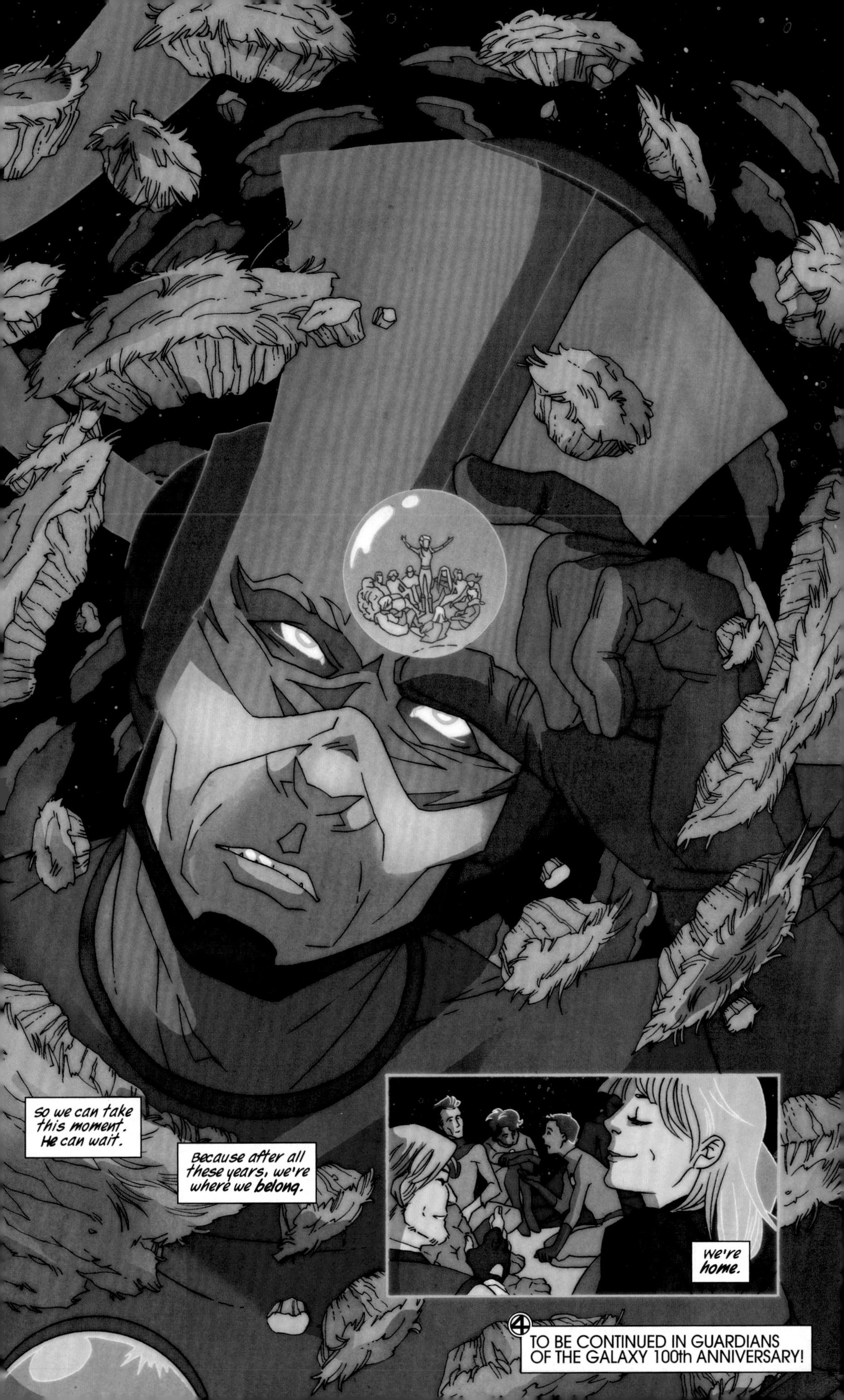
So we can take this moment. He can wait.
Because after all these years, we're where we belong.
We're home.
TO BE CONTINUED IN GUARDIANS OF THE GALAXY 100th ANNIVERSARY!

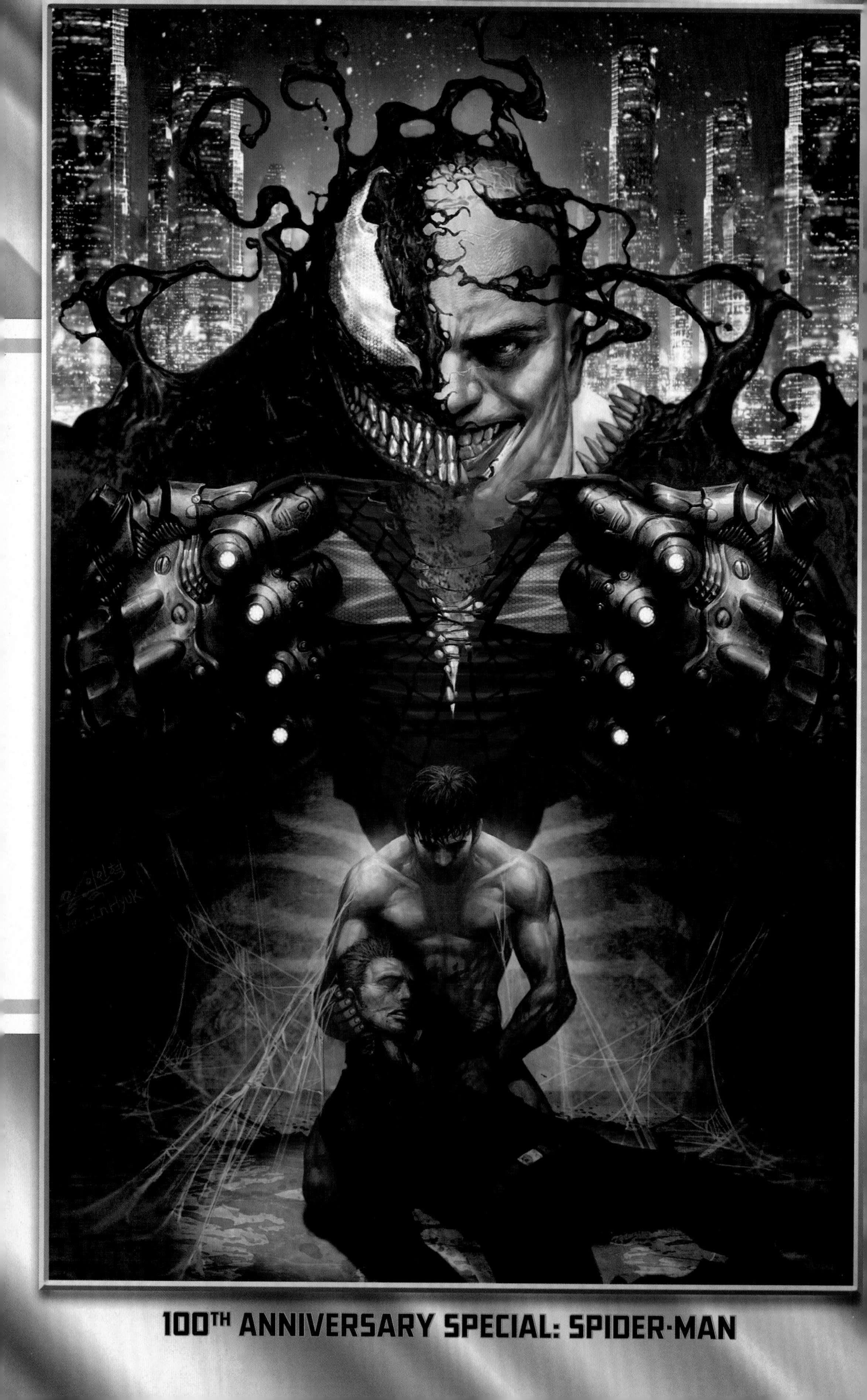

100TH ANNIVERSARY SPECIAL: SPIDER-MAN

DISGUSTED BY THE MAN HE HAD BECOME INSIDE THE TECHNO-SYMBIOTE SUIT, SPIDER-MAN TRIED TO DESTROY IT. BUT THE SUIT'S FORMER WEARER, EDDIE BROCK, WANTED THE SUIT BACK FOR HIMSELF. AFTER A STRUGGLE, THE TWO AGREED THAT THE SUIT SHOULD BE DESTROYED, BUT BEFORE THEY COULD COMPLETE THEIR PLAN THEY WERE KNOCKED UNCONSCIOUS BY AN UNKNOWN ASSAILANT. THEY CAME TO IN THE OFFICE OF WILSON FISK, A.K.A. THE KINGPIN. BEFORE EITHER SPIDER-MAN OR EDDIE KNEW WHAT WAS HAPPENING, THE KINGPIN SHOT EDDIE.

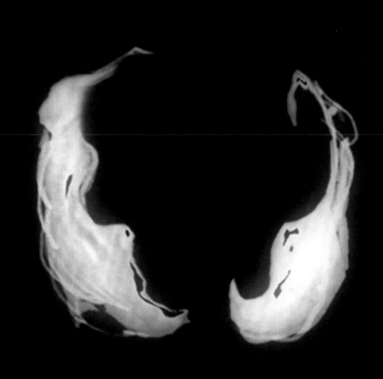

GREAT POWER
PART 8 OF 8

SEAN RYAN
WRITER

IN-HYUK LEE
ART

VC'S CLAYTON COWLES
LETTERER

IN-HYUK LEE
COVER

ALEXANDER LOZANO
VARIANT COVER

JAKE THOMAS
EDITOR

NICK LOWE
SENIOR EDITOR

AXEL ALONSO
EDITOR IN CHIEF

JOE QUESADA
CHIEF CREATIVE OFFICER

DAN BUCKLEY
PUBLISHER

ALAN FINE
EXECUTIVE EDITOR

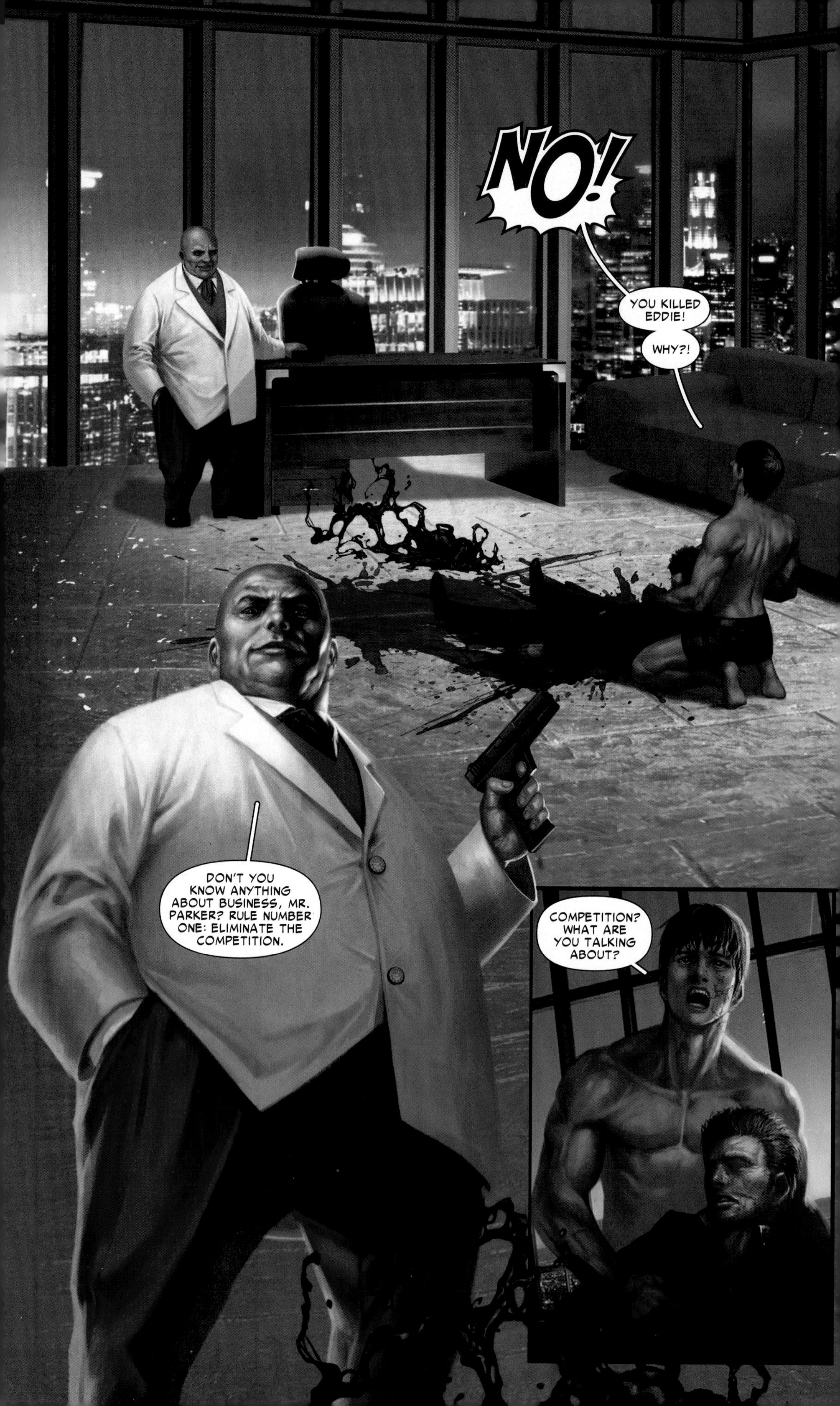
NO!
YOU KILLED EDDIE!
WHY?!
DON'T YOU KNOW ANYTHING ABOUT BUSINESS, MR. PARKER? RULE NUMBER ONE: ELIMINATE THE COMPETITION.
COMPETITION? WHAT ARE YOU TALKING ABOUT?

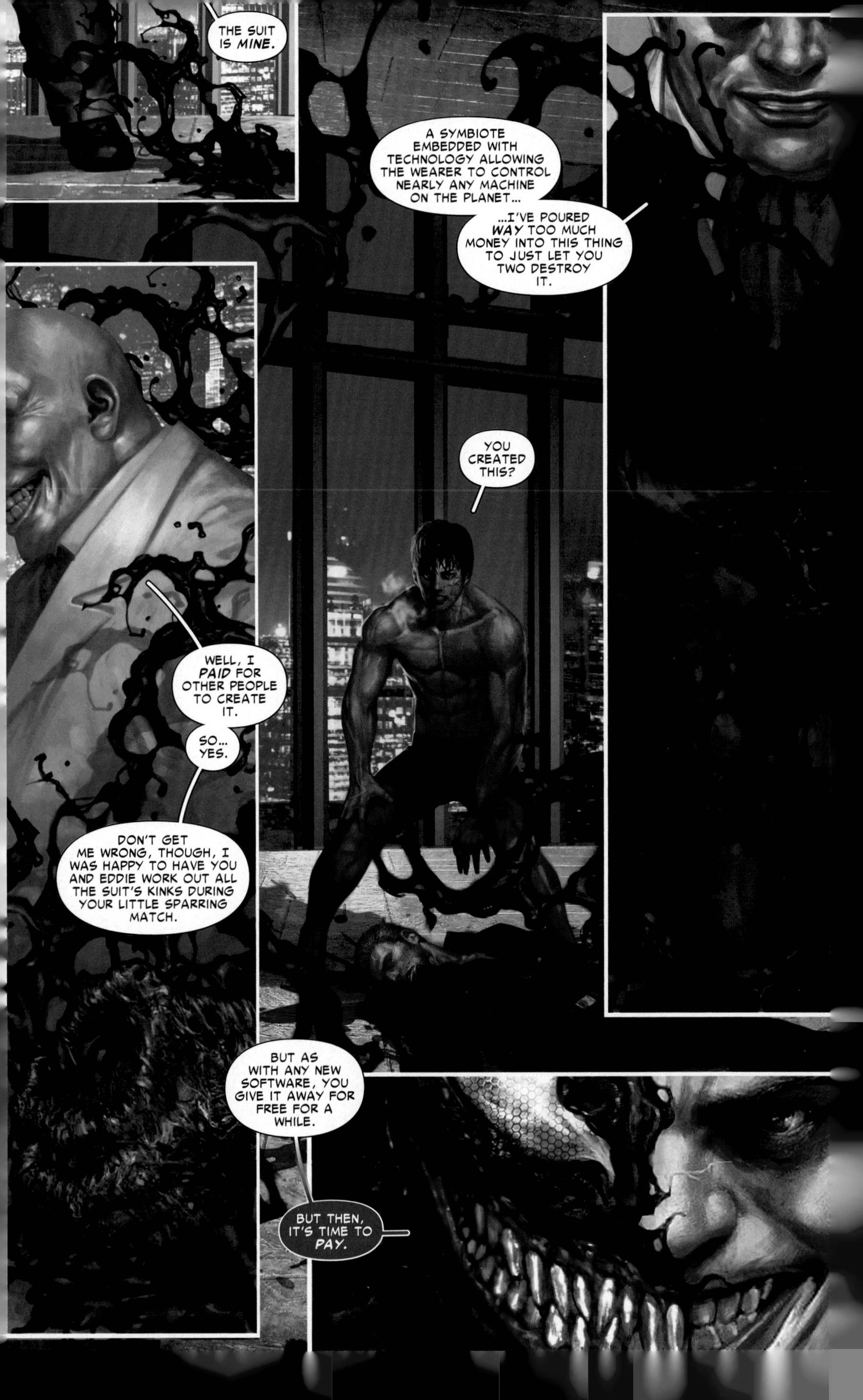
THE SUIT IS MINE.
A SYMBIOTE EMBEDDED WITH TECHNOLOGY ALLOWING THE WEARER TO CONTROL NEARLY ANY MACHINE ON THE PLANET...
...I'VE POURED WAY TOO MUCH MONEY INTO THIS THING TO JUST LET YOU TWO DESTROY IT.
YOU CREATED THIS?
WELL, I PAID FOR OTHER PEOPLE TO CREATE IT.
SO... YES.
DON'T GET ME WRONG, THOUGH, I WAS HAPPY TO HAVE YOU AND EDDIE WORK OUT ALL THE SUIT'S KINKS DURING YOUR LITTLE SPARRING MATCH.
BUT AS WITH ANY NEW SOFTWARE, YOU GIVE IT AWAY FOR FREE FOR A WHILE.
BUT THEN, IT'S TIME TO PAY.

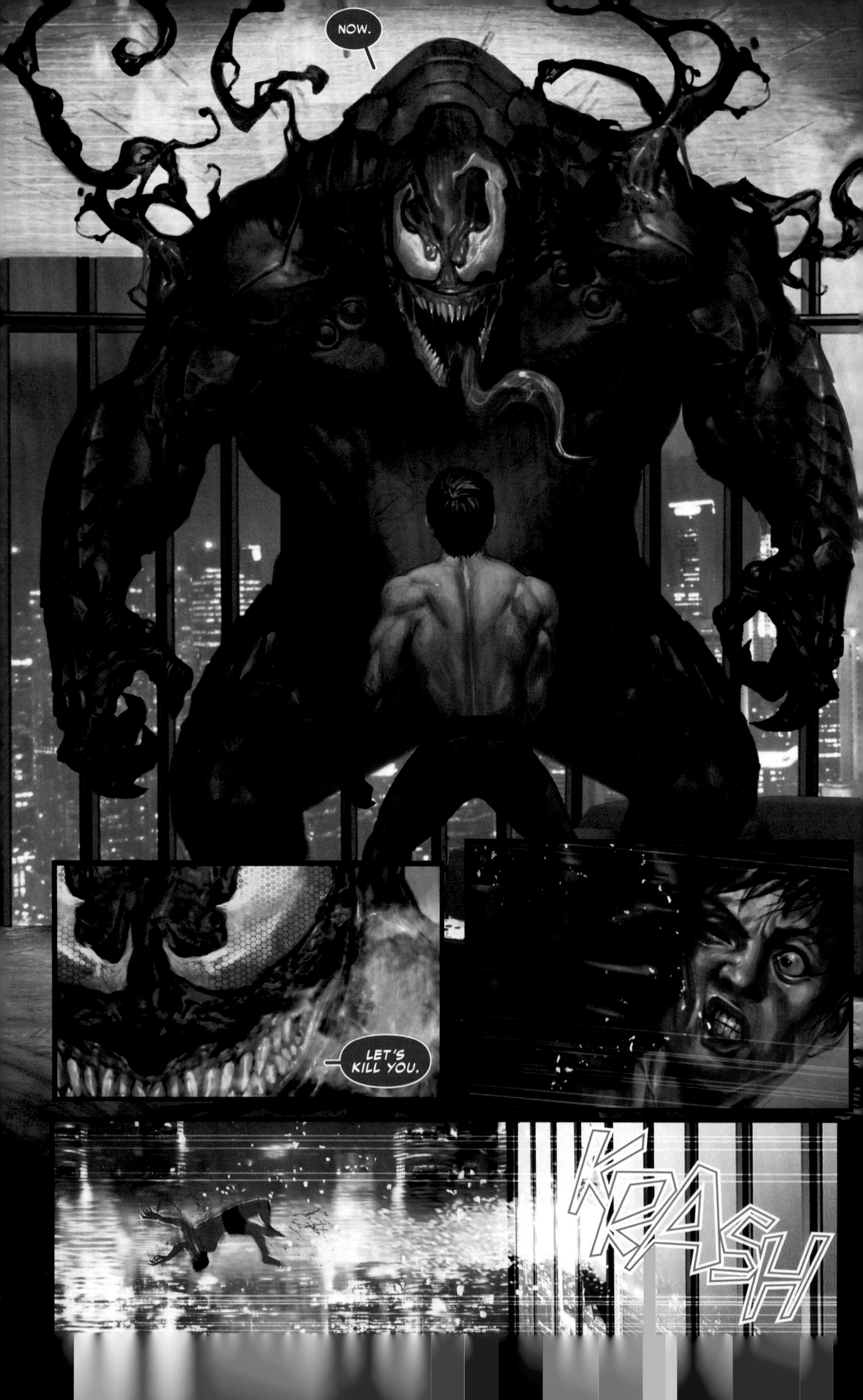
NOW.
LET'S KILL YOU.
KRASH

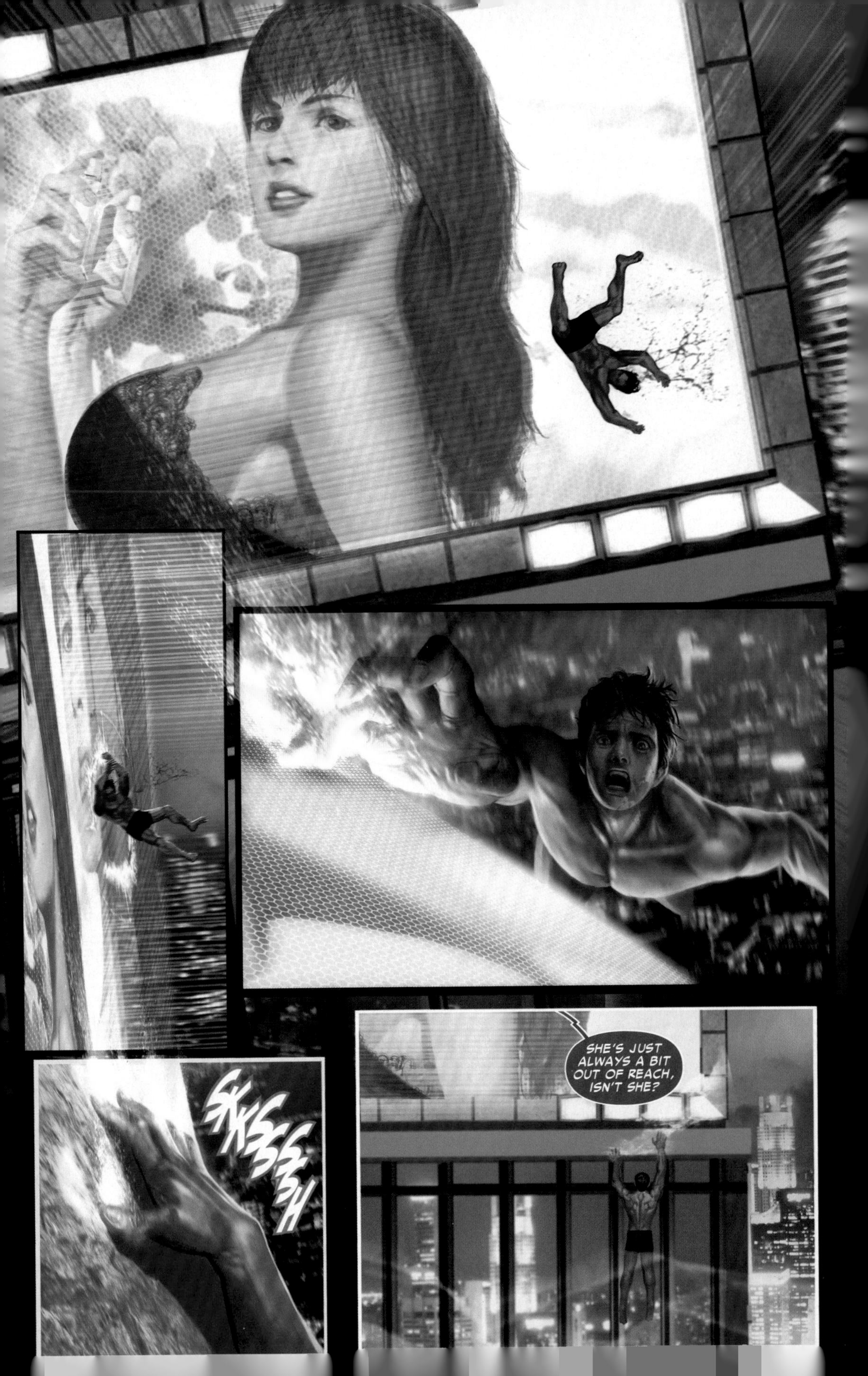
SKKSSSSH!!
SHE'S JUST ALWAYS A BIT OUT OF REACH, ISN'T SHE?

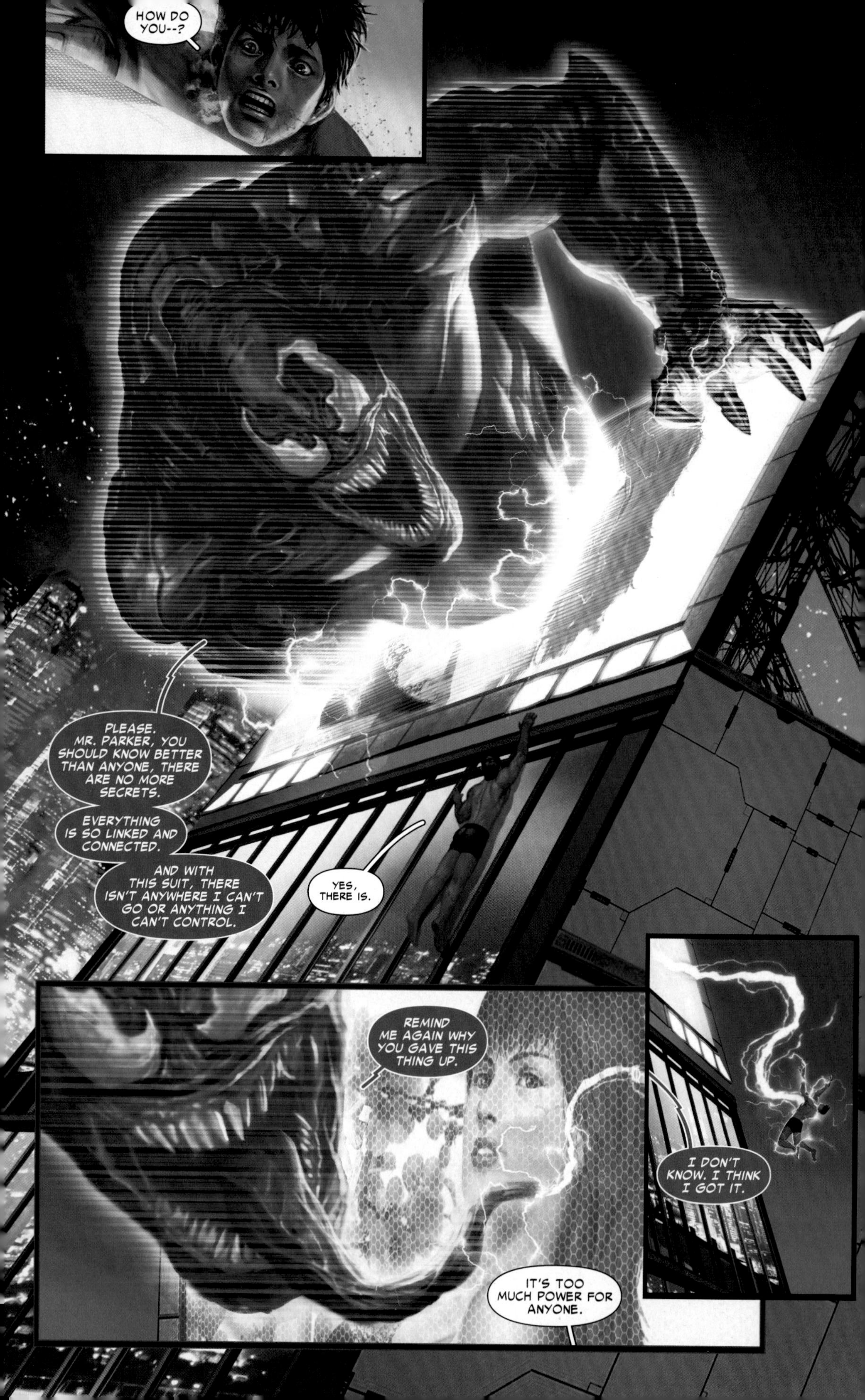
HOW DO YOU--?
PLEASE. MR. PARKER, YOU SHOULD KNOW BETTER THAN ANYONE, THERE ARE NO MORE SECRETS.
EVERYTHING IS SO LINKED AND CONNECTED.
AND WITH THIS SUIT, THERE ISN'T ANYWHERE I CAN'T GO OR ANYTHING I CAN'T CONTROL.
YES, THERE IS.
REMIND ME AGAIN WHY YOU GAVE THIS THING UP.
IT'S TOO MUCH POWER FOR ANYONE.
I DON'T KNOW. I THINK I GOT IT.

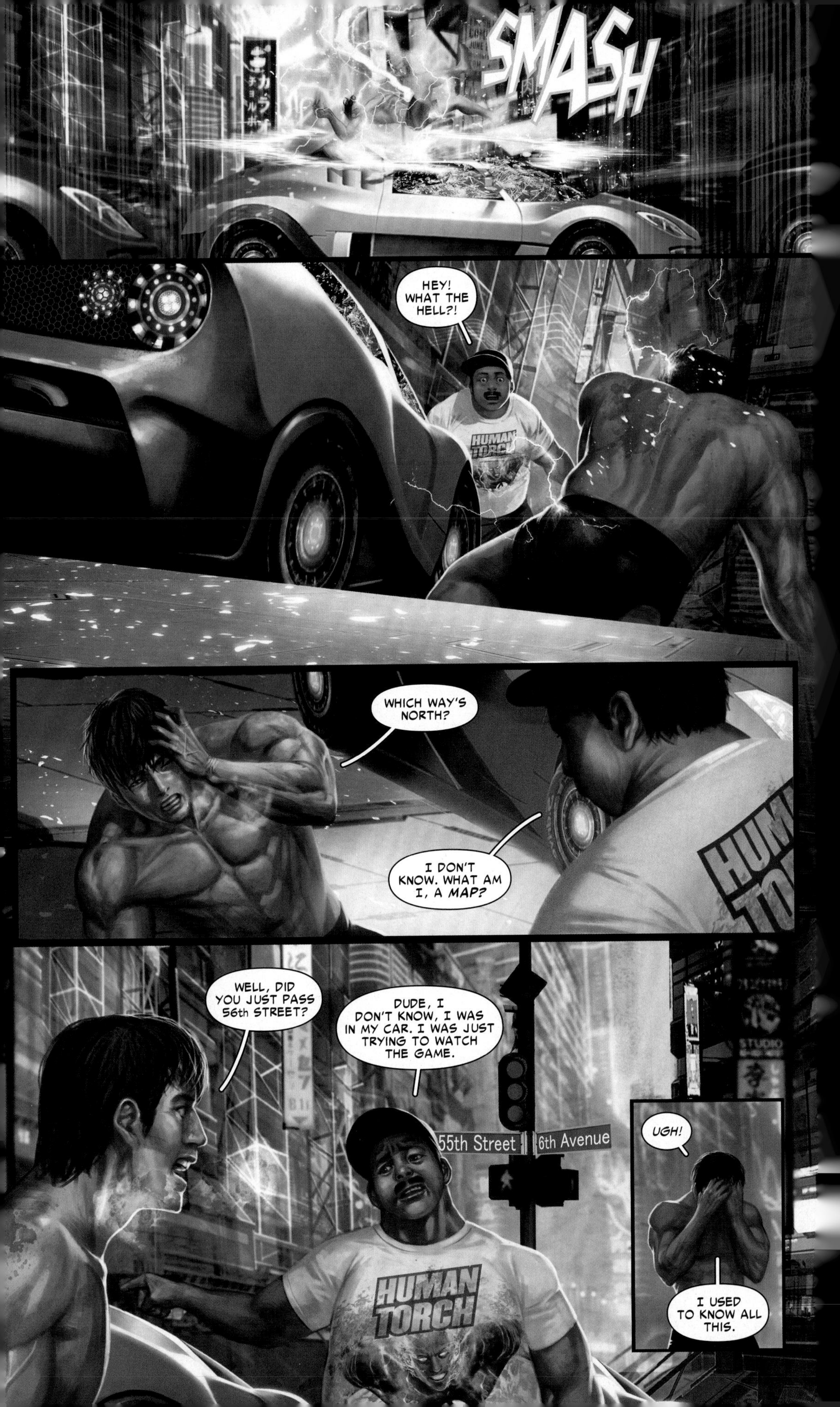
SMASH
HEY! WHAT THE HELL?!
HUMAN TORCH
WHICH WAY'S NORTH?
I DON'T KNOW. WHAT AM I, A *MAP?*
WELL, DID YOU JUST PASS 56th STREET?
DUDE, I DON'T KNOW, I WAS IN MY CAR. I WAS JUST TRYING TO WATCH THE GAME.
55th Street
6th Avenue
HUMAN TORCH
UGH!
I USED TO KNOW ALL THIS.

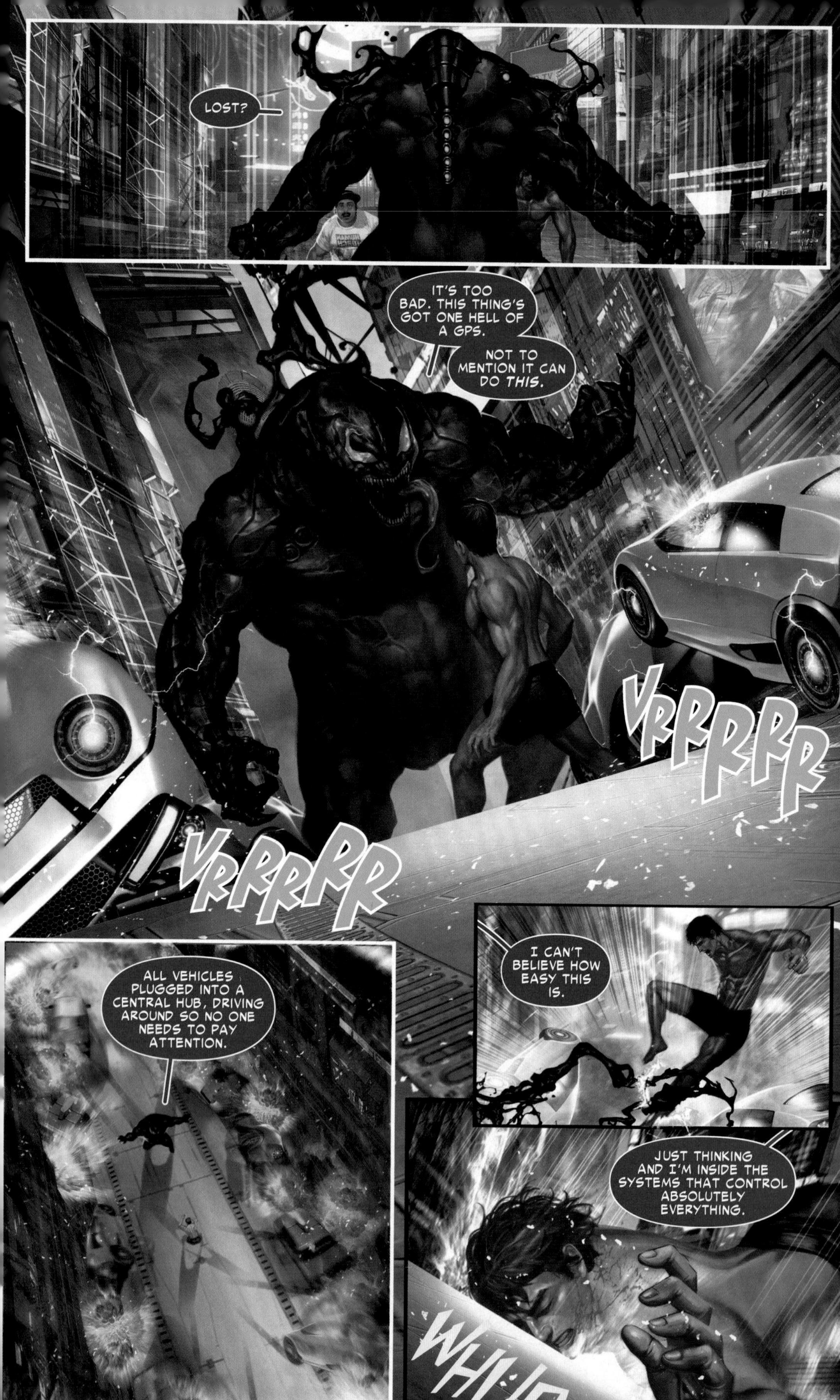
LOST?
IT'S TOO BAD. THIS THING'S GOT ONE HELL OF A GPS.
NOT TO MENTION IT CAN DO *THIS*.
VRRRRR
VRRRRR
ALL VEHICLES PLUGGED INTO A CENTRAL HUB, DRIVING AROUND SO NO ONE NEEDS TO PAY ATTENTION.
I CAN'T BELIEVE HOW EASY THIS IS.
JUST THINKING AND I'M INSIDE THE SYSTEMS THAT CONTROL ABSOLUTELY EVERYTHING.
WHUP

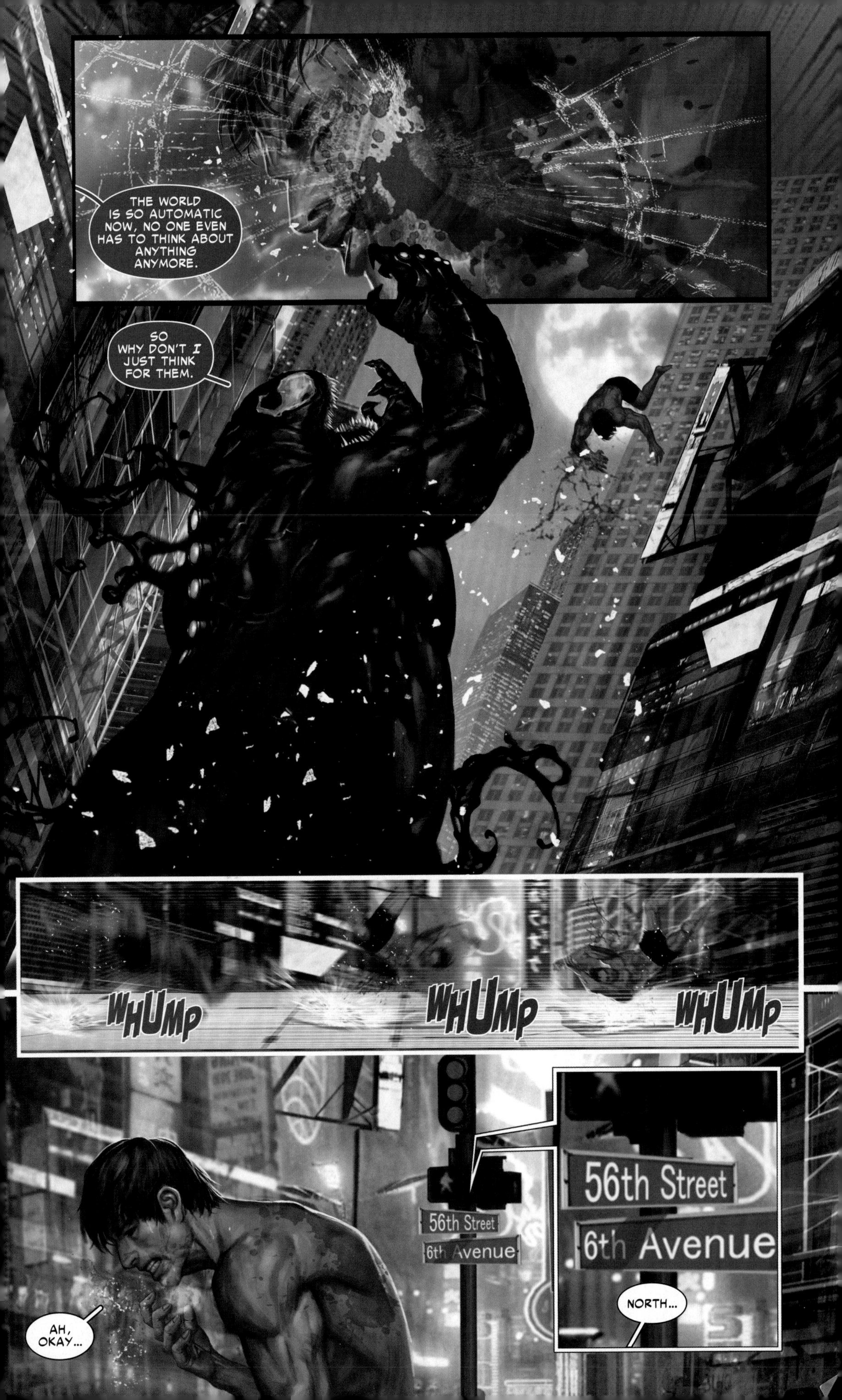
THE WORLD IS SO AUTOMATIC NOW, NO ONE EVEN HAS TO THINK ABOUT ANYTHING ANYMORE.
SO WHY DON'T I JUST THINK FOR THEM.
WHUMP
WHUMP
WHUMP
56th Street
6th Avenue
56th Street
6th Avenue
NORTH...
AH, OKAY...

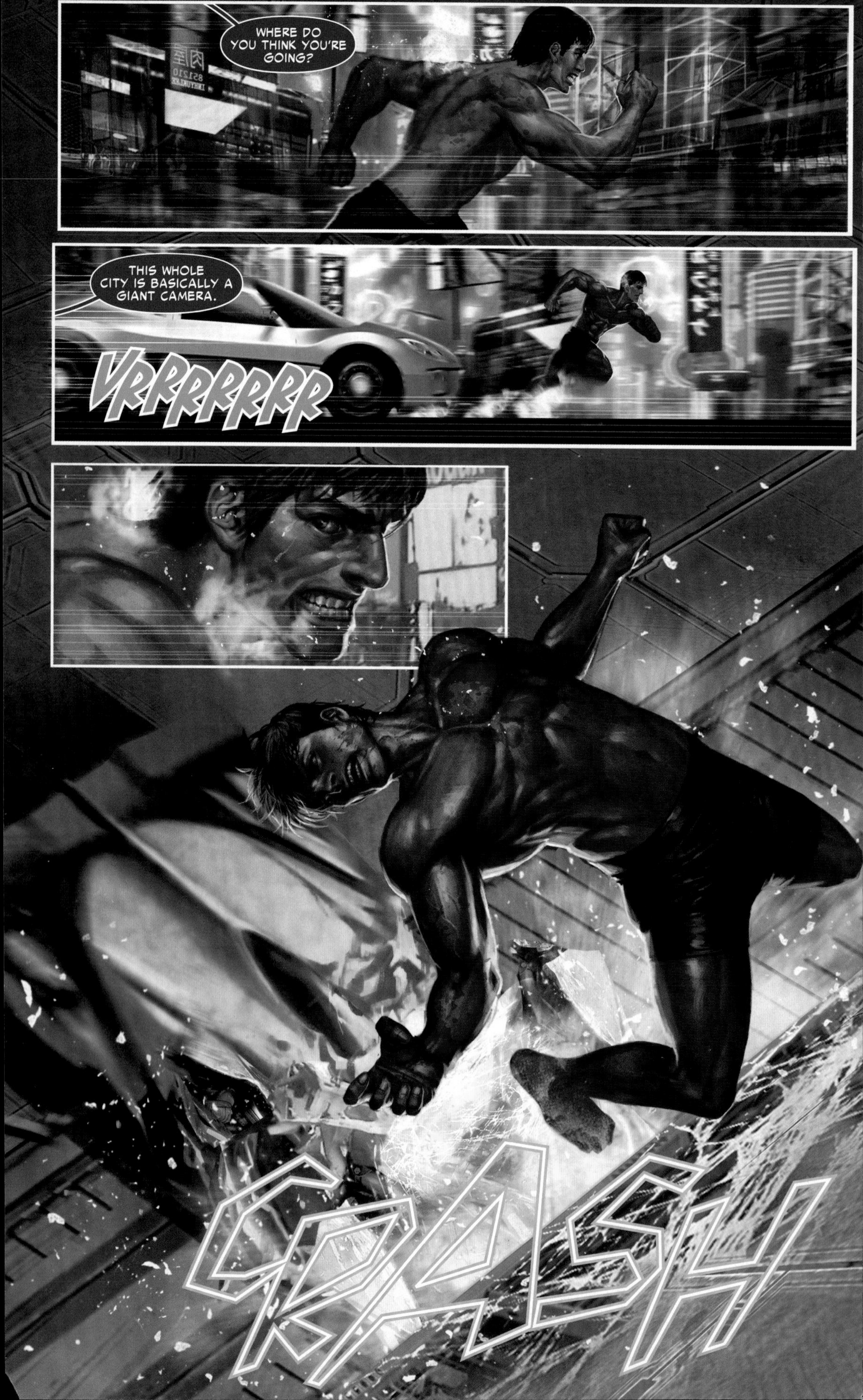
WHERE DO YOU THINK YOU'RE GOING?
THIS WHOLE CITY IS BASICALLY A GIANT CAMERA.
VRRRRRRR
CRASH

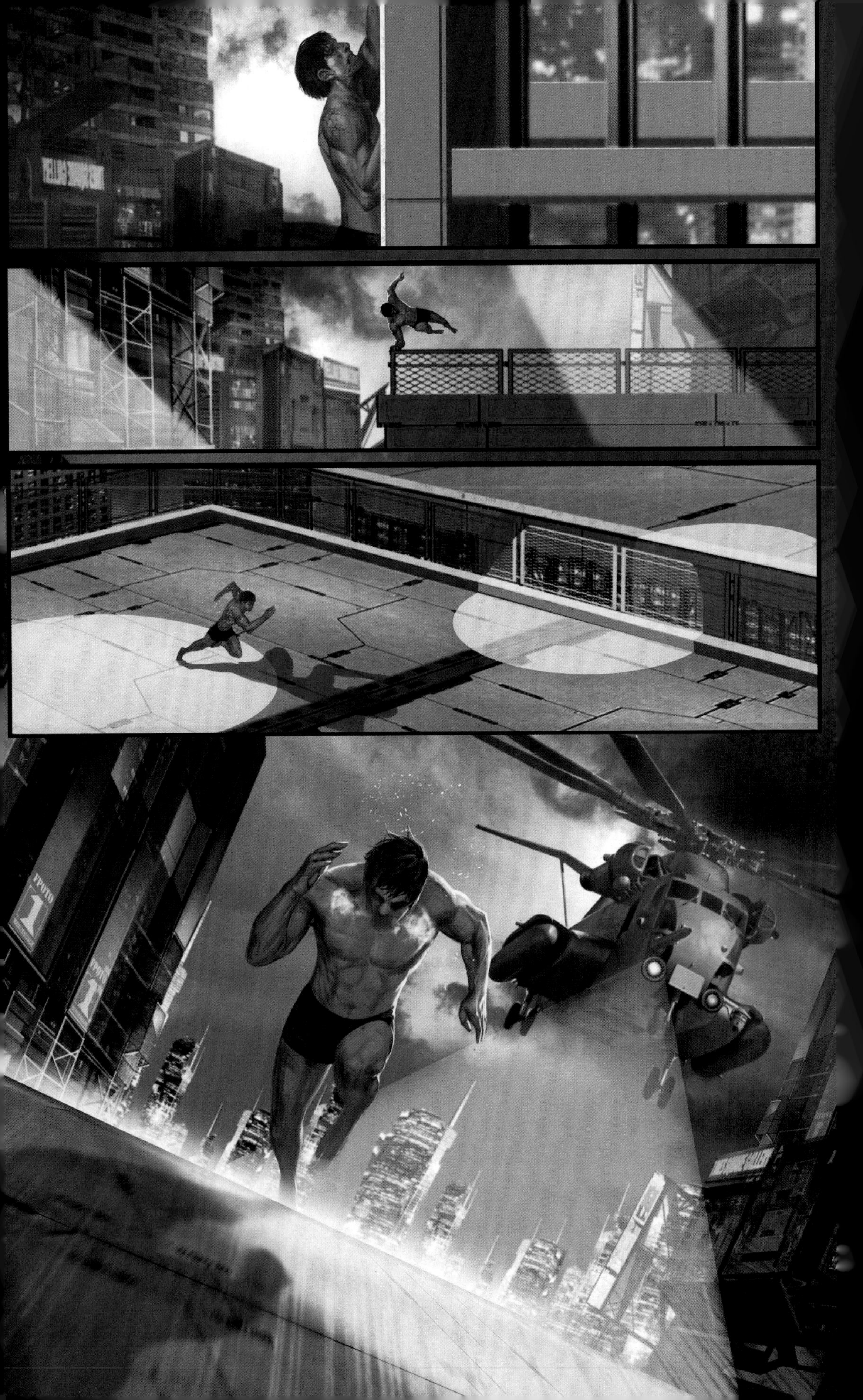

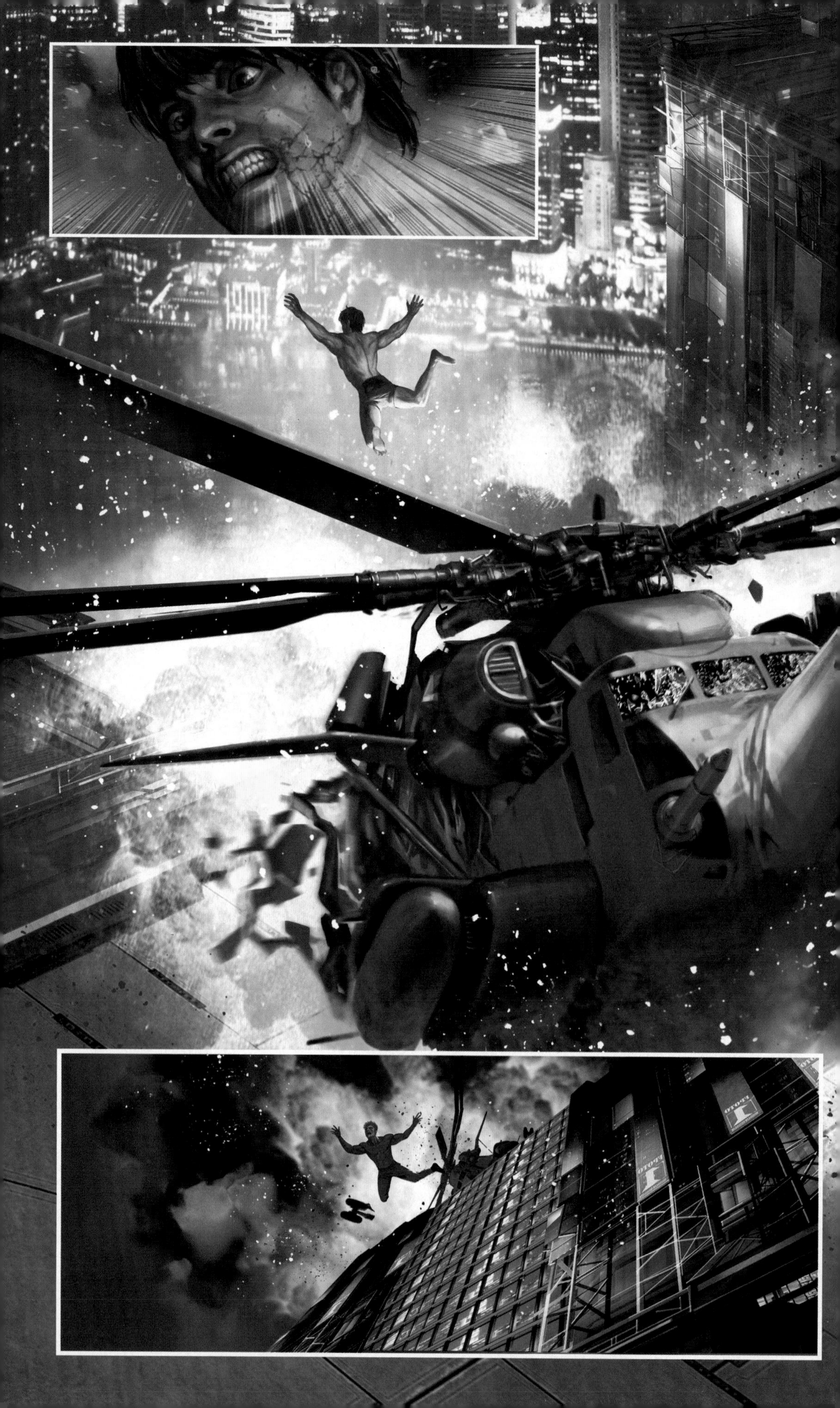

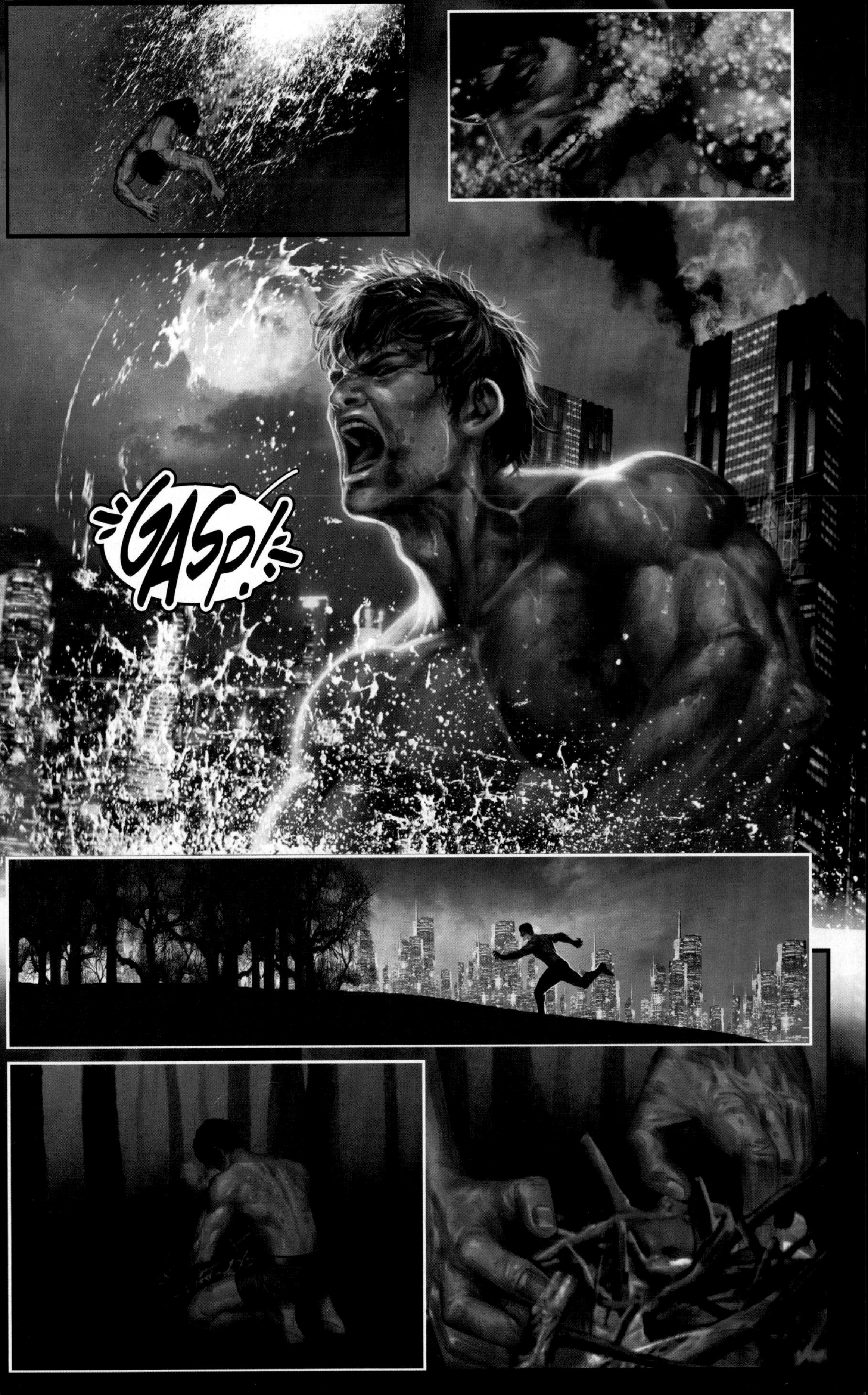
GASP!

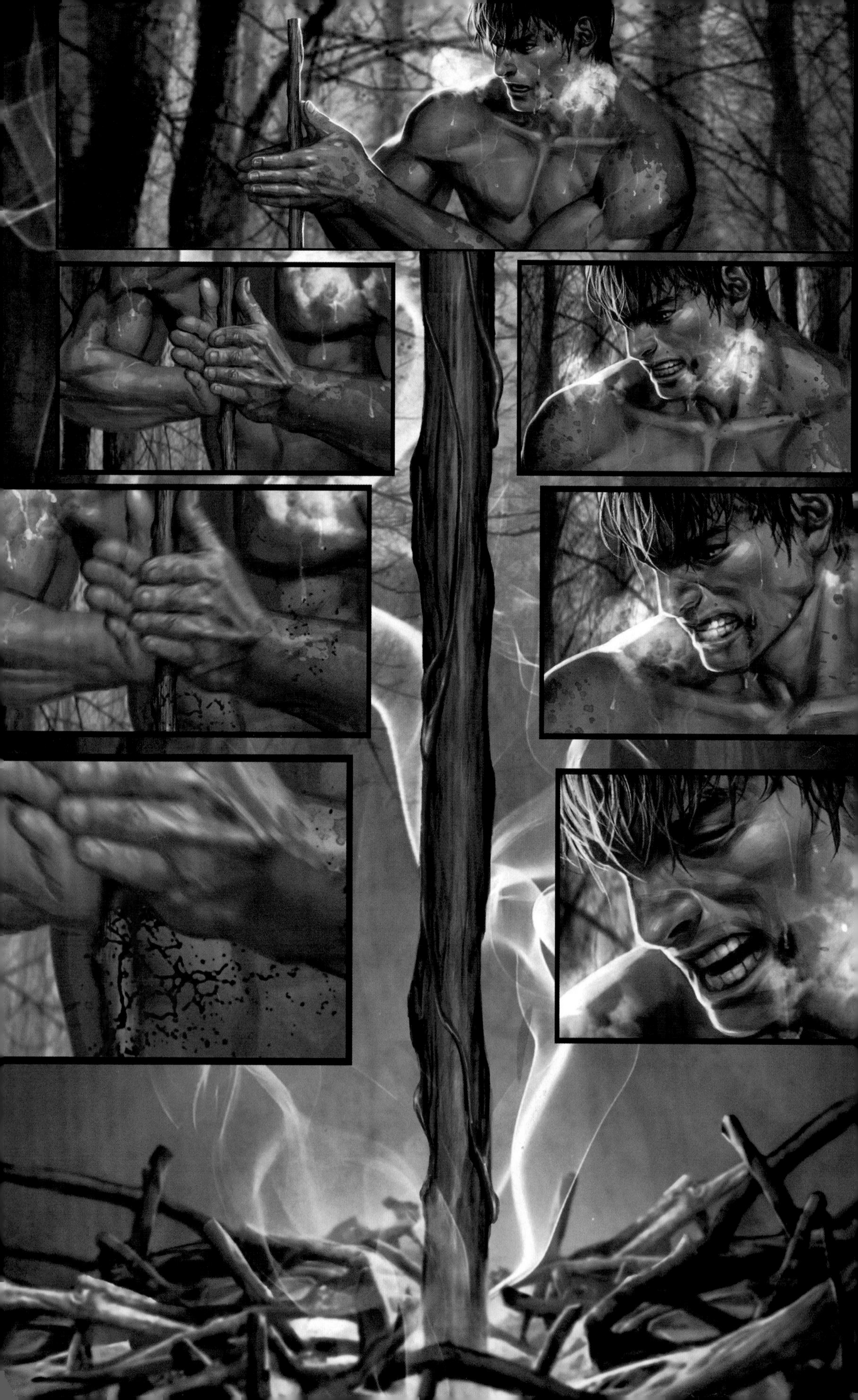

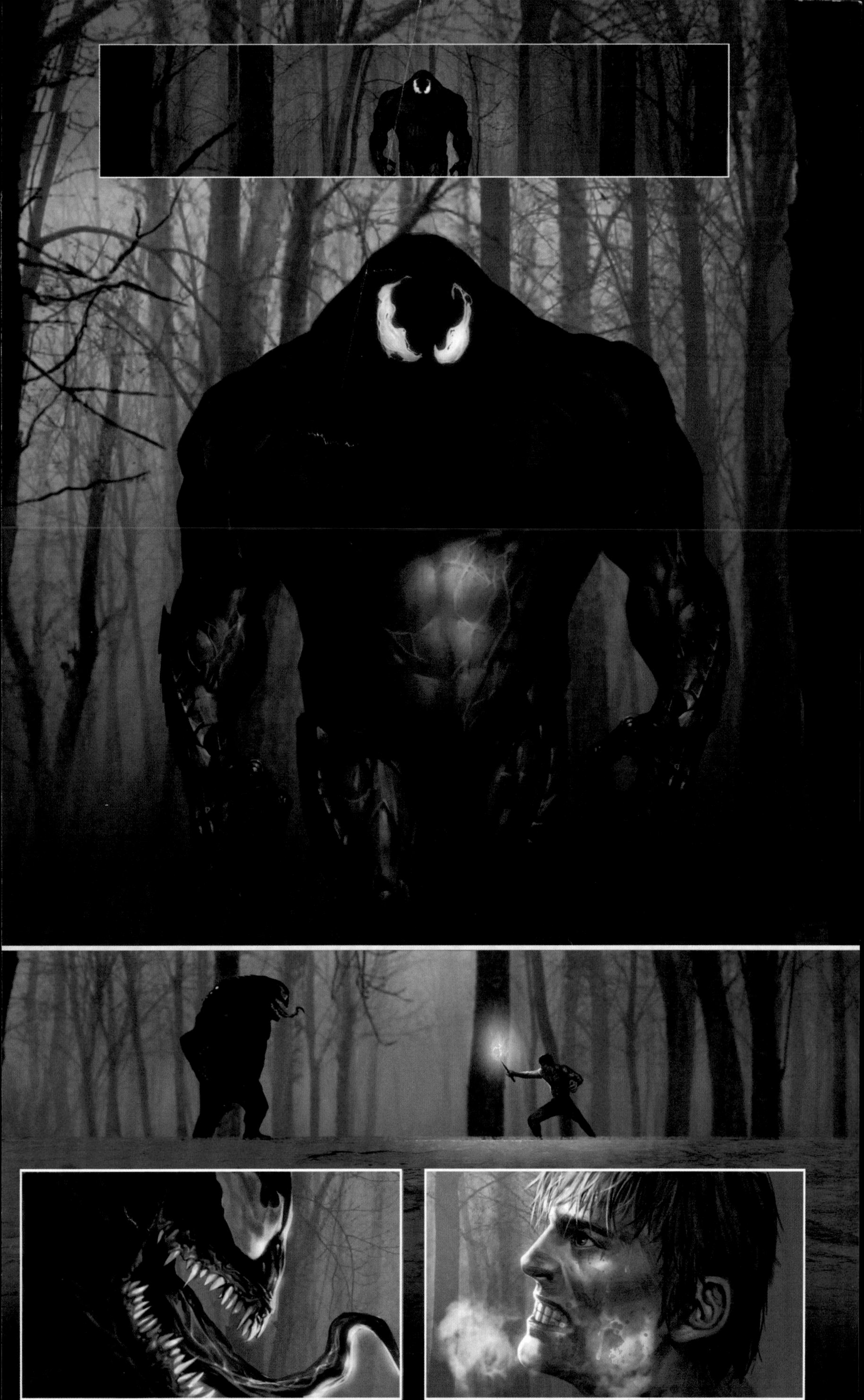

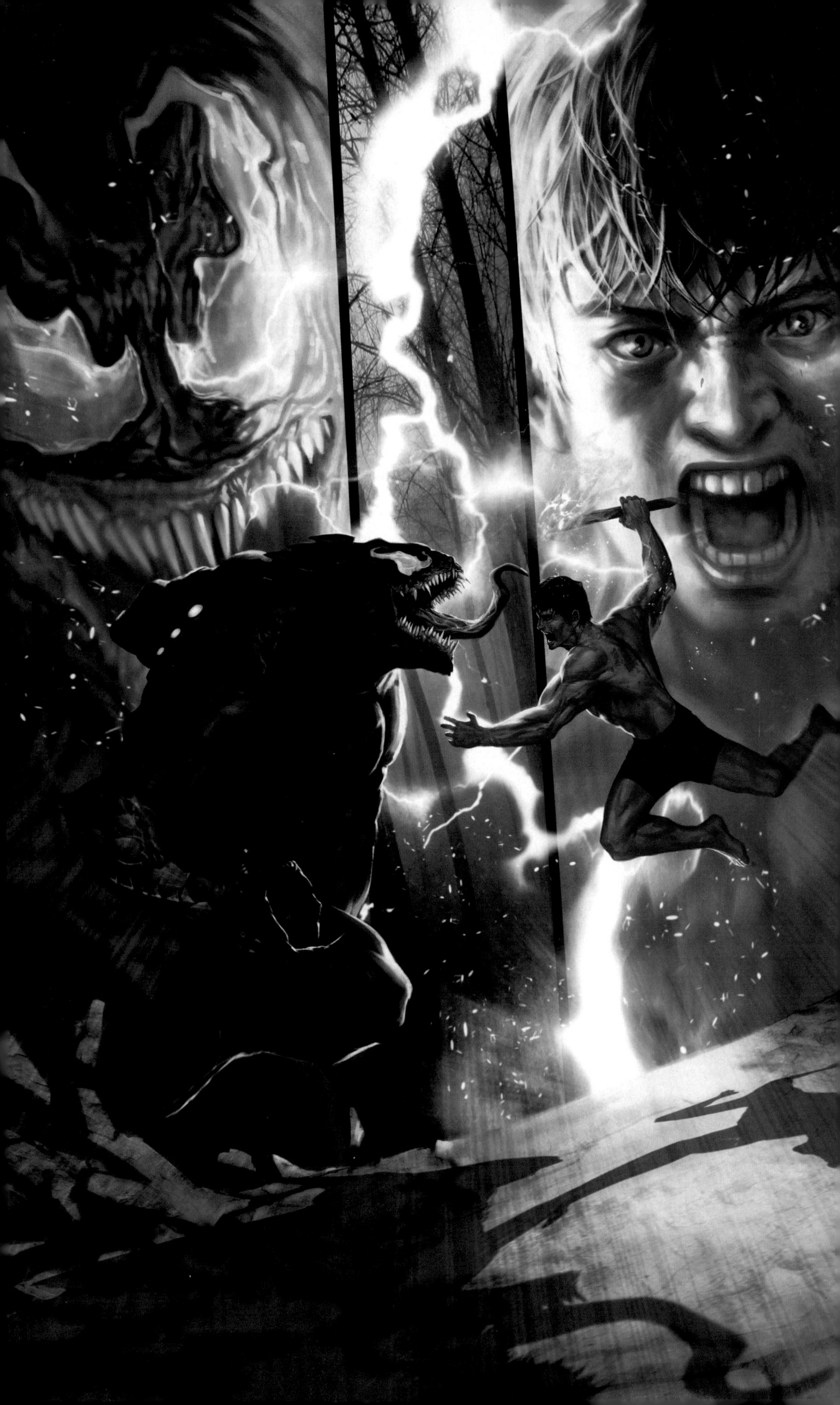

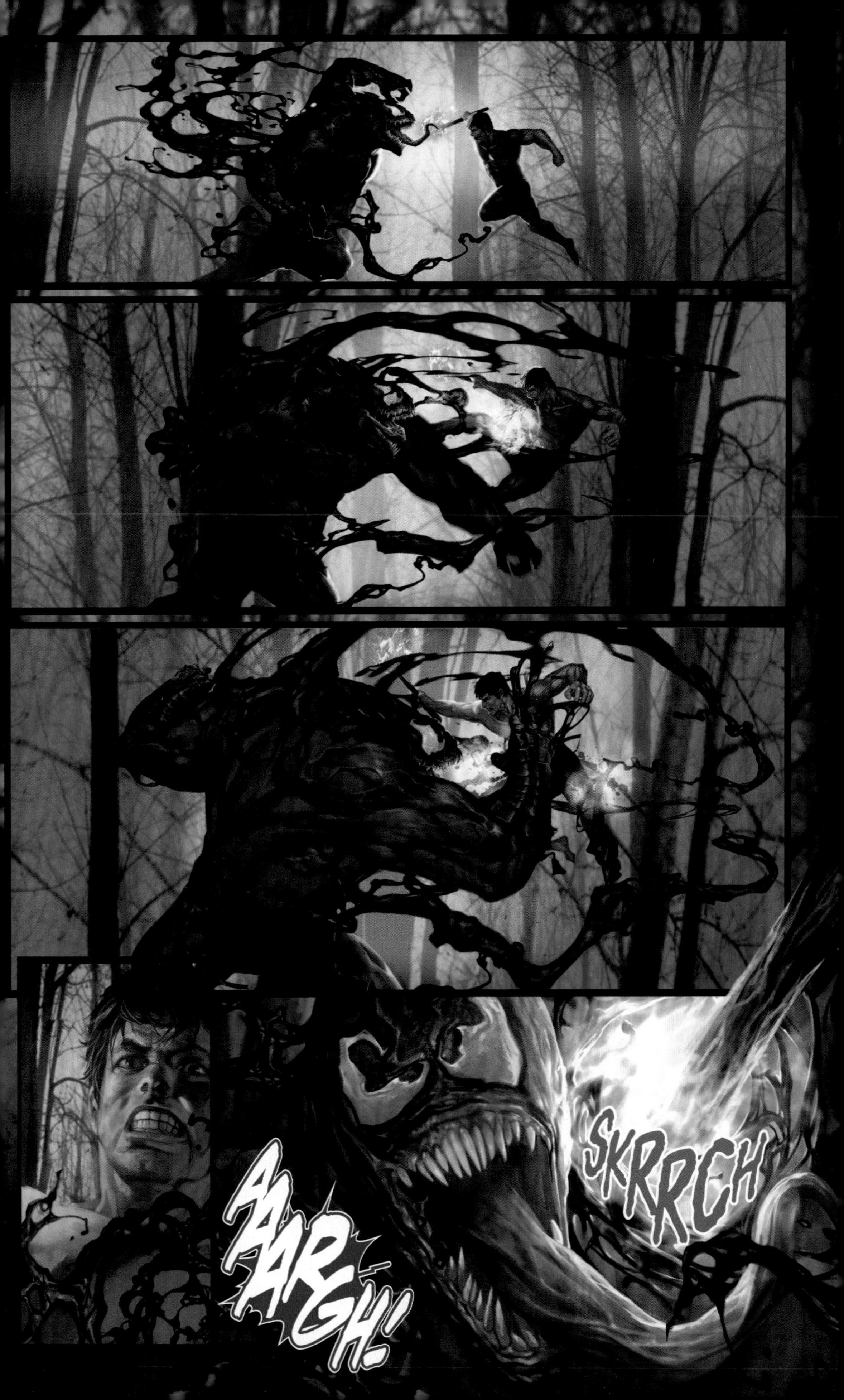
AAARGH!
SKRRCH

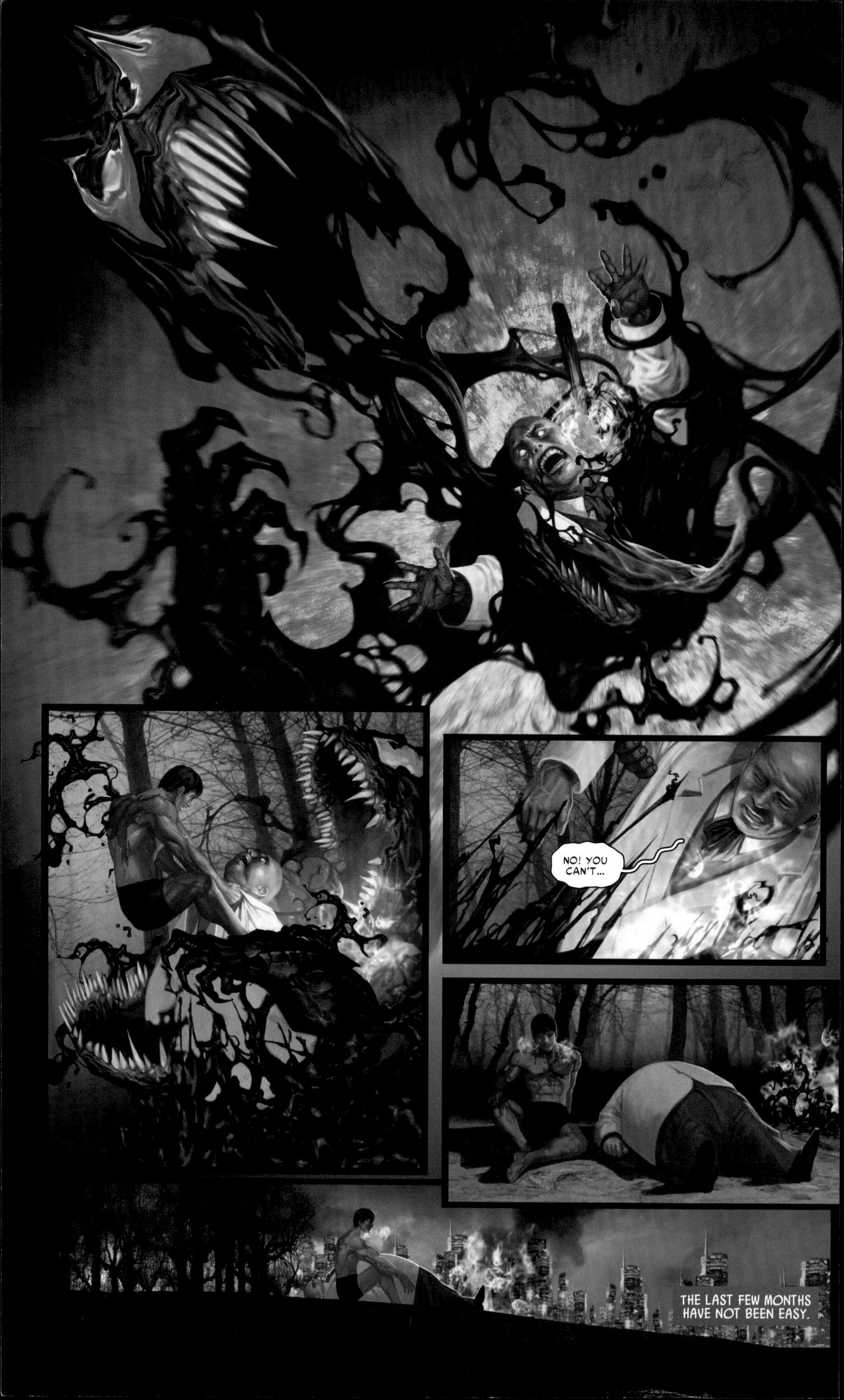
NO! YOU CAN'T...
THE LAST FEW MONTHS HAVE NOT BEEN EASY.

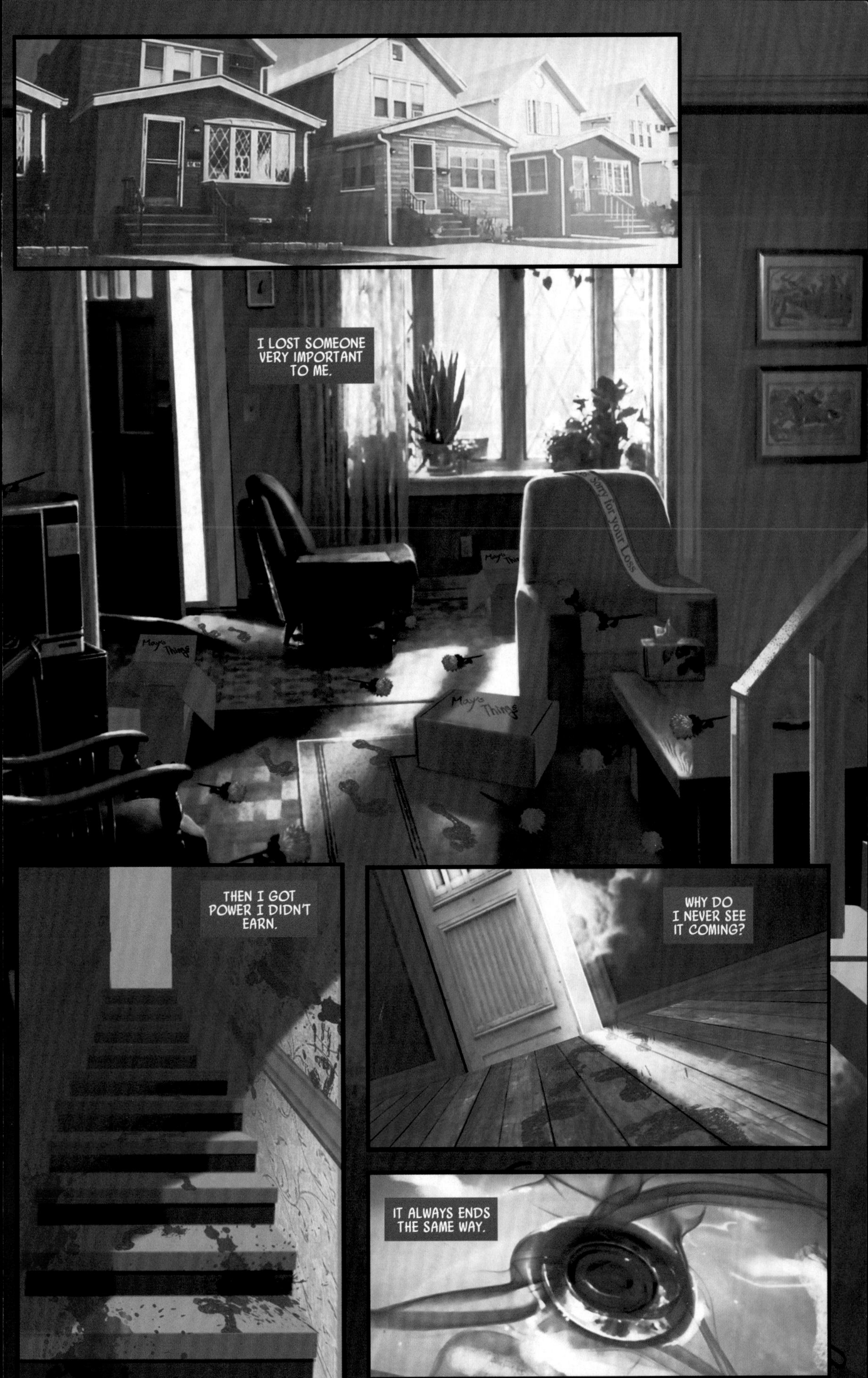
I LOST SOMEONE VERY IMPORTANT TO ME.
THEN I GOT POWER I DIDN'T EARN.
WHY DO I NEVER SEE IT COMING?
IT ALWAYS ENDS THE SAME WAY.

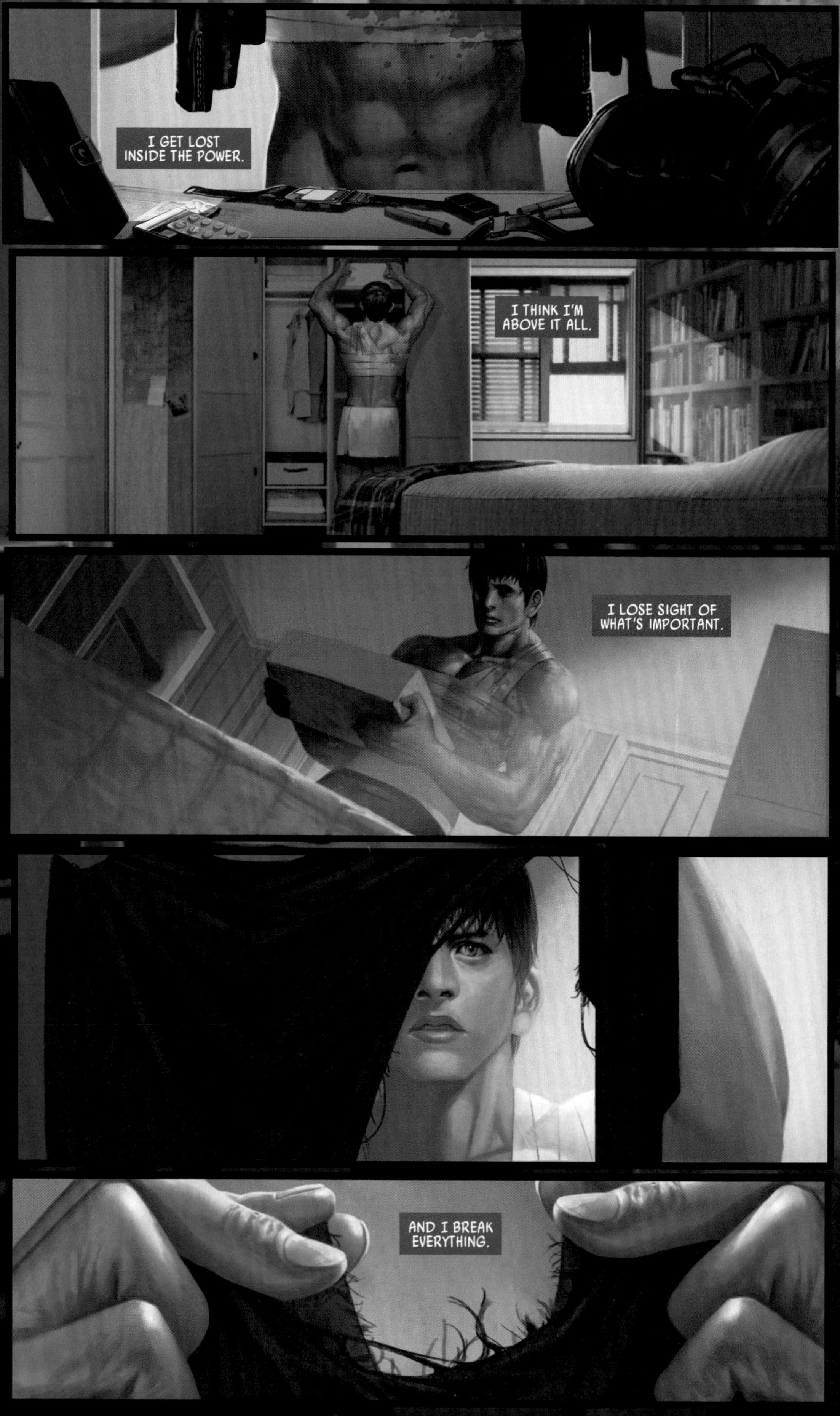
I GET LOST INSIDE THE POWER.
I THINK I'M ABOVE IT ALL.
I LOSE SIGHT OF WHAT'S IMPORTANT.
AND I BREAK EVERYTHING.

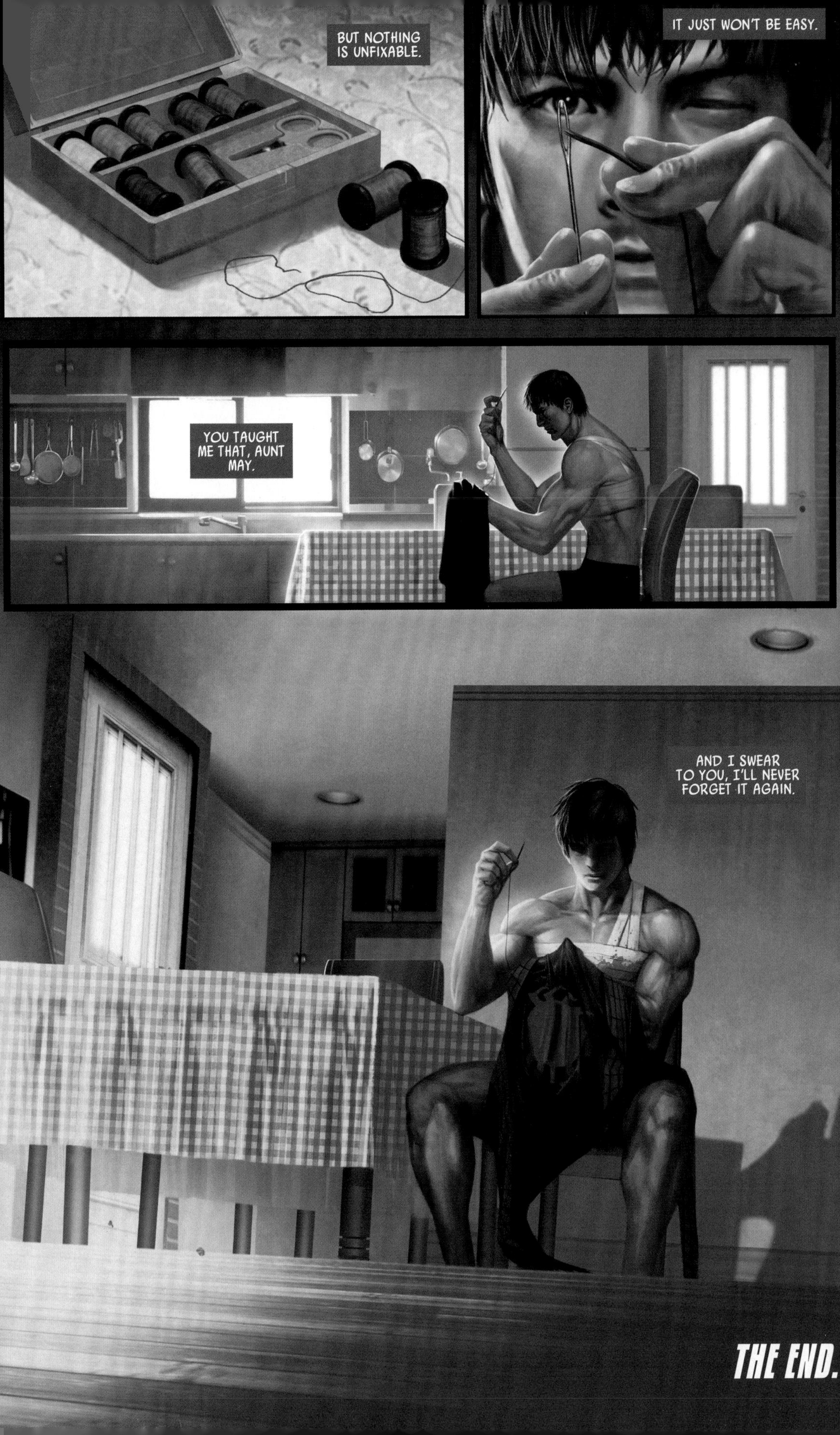
BUT NOTHING IS UNFIXABLE.
IT JUST WON'T BE EASY.
YOU TAUGHT ME THAT, AUNT MAY.
AND I SWEAR TO YOU, I'LL NEVER FORGET IT AGAIN.
THE END.

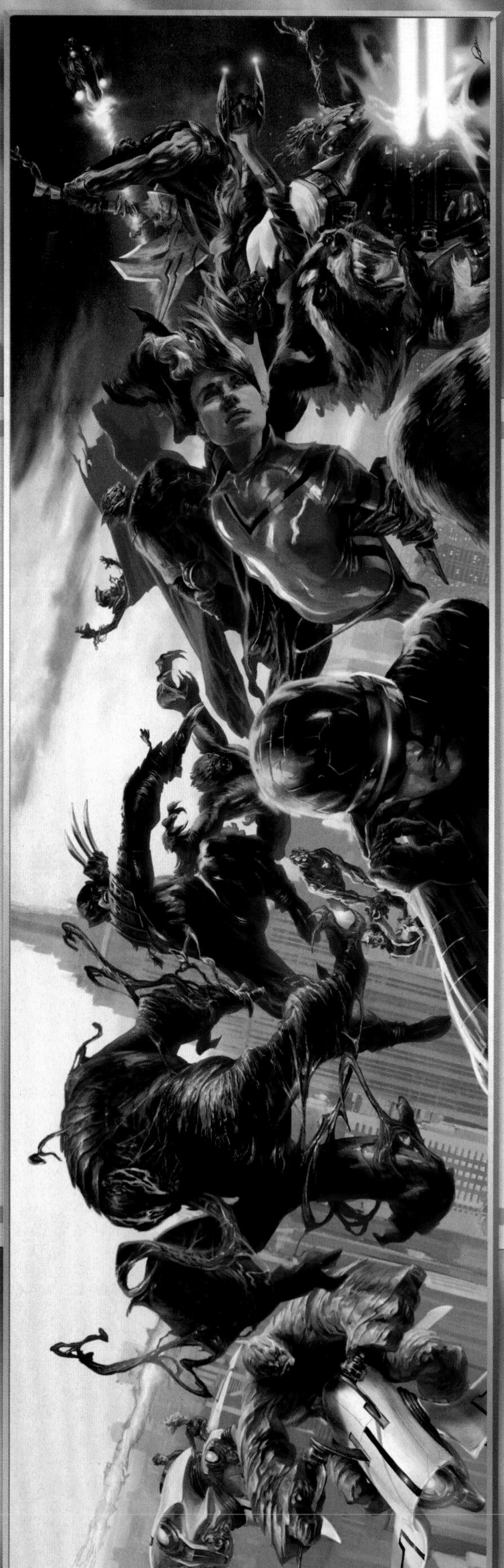

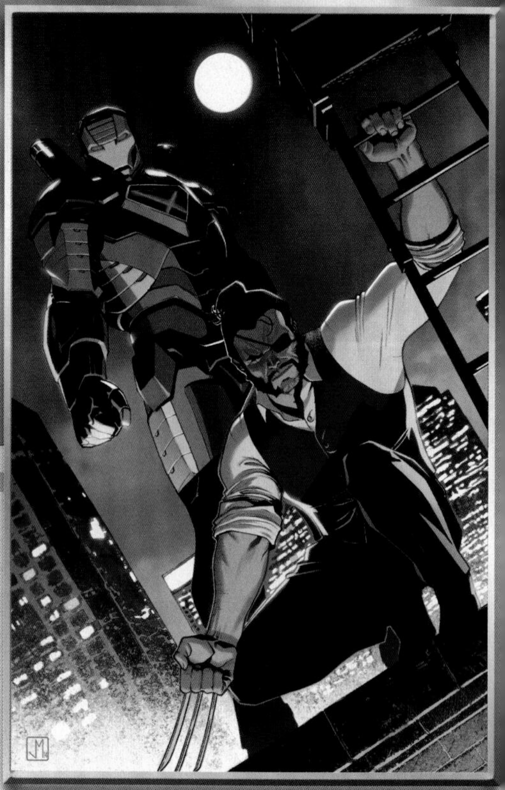

ABOVE: X-MEN VARIANT COVER BY JORGE MOLINA
LEFT: COMBINED VARIANT COVERS BY ALEXANDER LOZANO
BELOW: GUARDIANS OF THE GALAXY VARIANT COVER BY GREG HORN

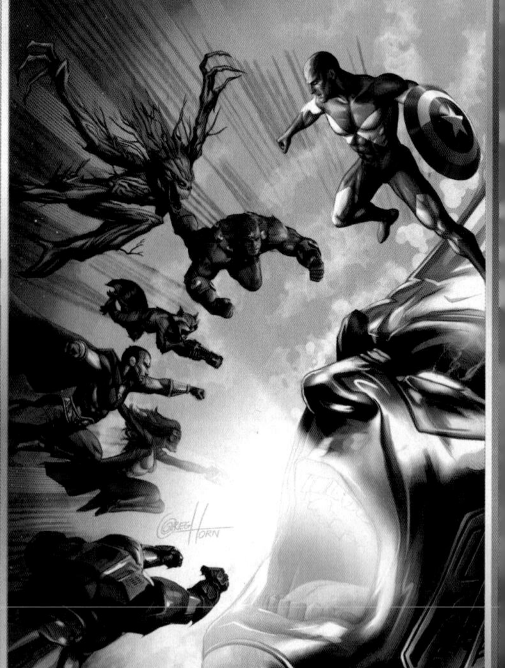

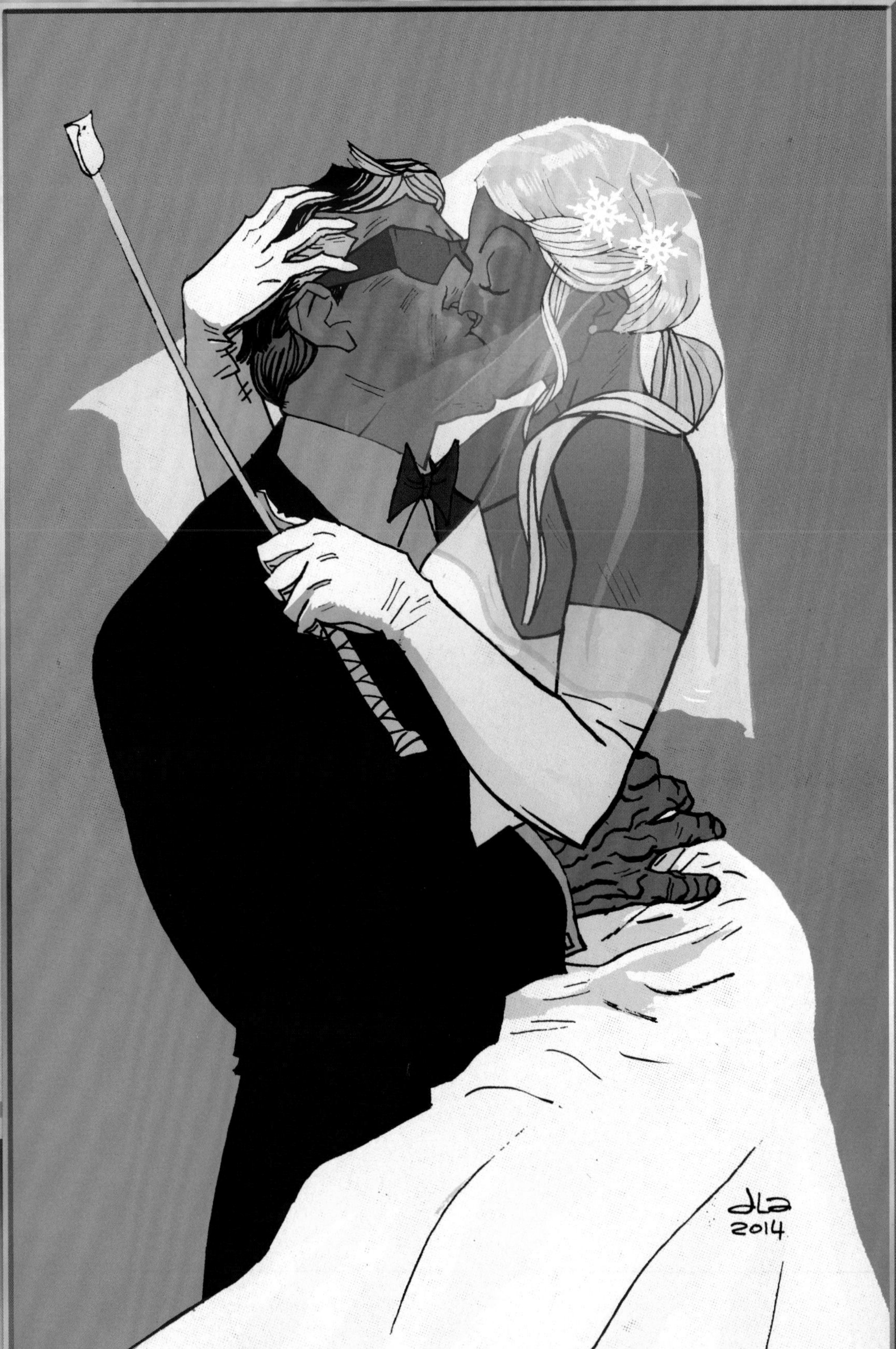
dla
2014

100TH ANNIVERSARY SPECIAL: X-MEN

When Cyclops and his band of mutant revolutionaries destroyed the black hole growing at the heart of the Brookhaven National Laboratory's Large Hadron Collider, they saved the State of New York and were hailed as national heroes. On the wave of the pro-mutant sentiment that followed, Scott Summers, leader of the reunited X-Men, expanded his political agenda to include fighting for the rights of all people traditionally excluded from power. As the head of the Pro-Mutant Party, Scott was elected President of the United States. Yet the nation he has been chosen to lead remains dangerously divided. Funded by the new Hellfire Club, both the Sapien League and the Purifiers have been working to oust the X-Men from power, while the Eugenics Society fights to return America to what they claim is the traditional status quo. Despite this conflict, Scott finally tied the knot with his longtime on-again, off-again lover, Emma Frost. But an even more terrible threat is about to emerge—one that could destroy the X-Men, and possibly the world as we know it, forever.

ROBIN FURTH
WRITER

JASON MASTERS
ARTIST

JAMES CAMPBELL AND VERO GANDINI
COLORISTS

JASON LATOUR
COVER ARTIST

VC'S CORY PETIT
LETTERER

XANDER JAROWEY
EDITOR

MIKE MARTS
X-MEN GROUP EDITOR

AXEL ALONSO
EDITOR IN CHIEF

JOE QUESADA
CHIEF CREATIVE OFFICER

DAN BUCKLEY
PUBLISHER

ALAN FINE
EXECUTIVE PRODUCER

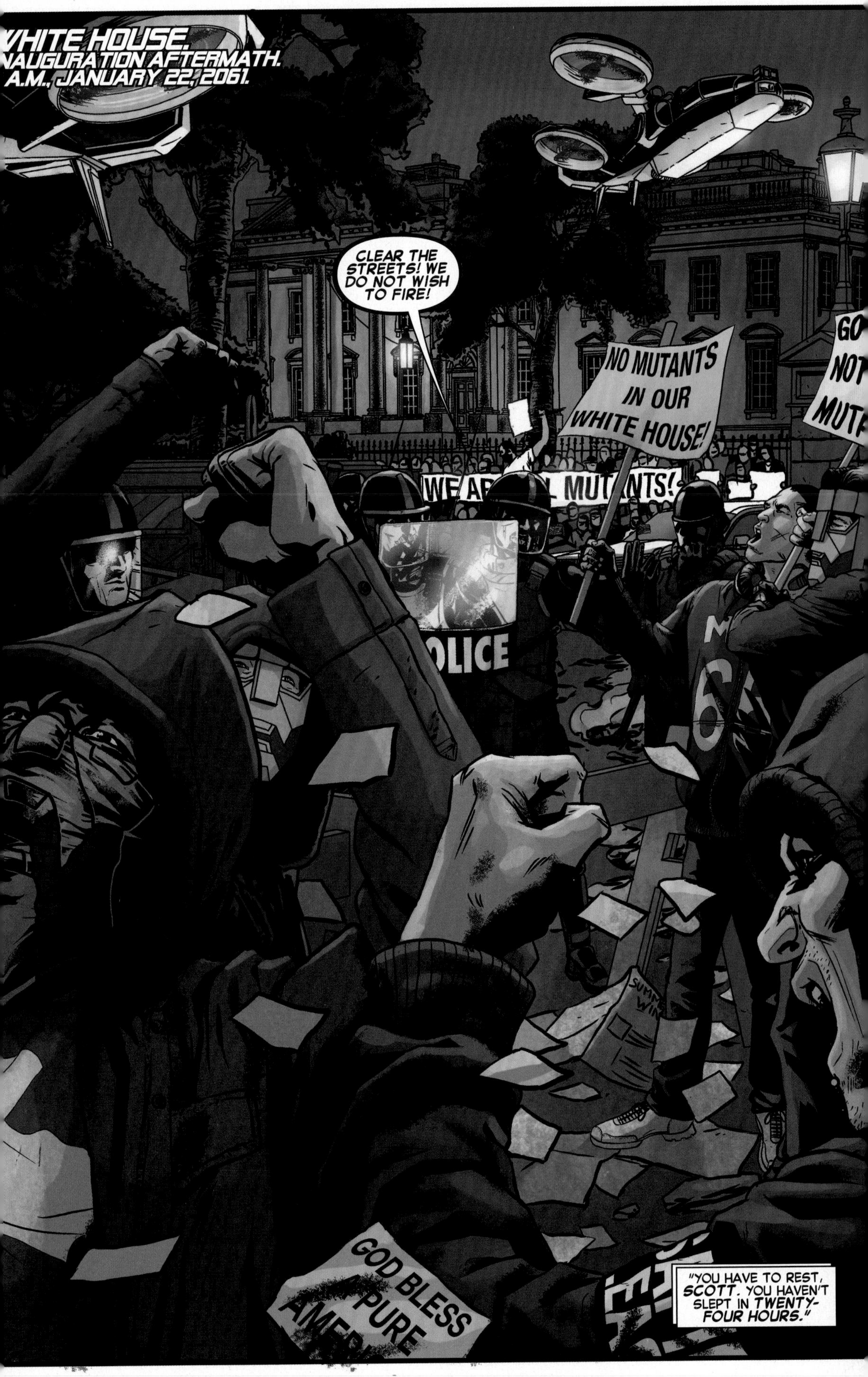

VHITE HOUSE.
NAUGURATION AFTERMATH.
A.M., JANUARY 22, 2061.
CLEAR THE STREETS! WE DO NOT WISH TO FIRE!
NO MUTANTS IN OUR WHITE HOUSE!
OLICE
GOD BLESS
PURE
"YOU HAVE TO REST, SCOTT. YOU HAVEN'T SLEPT IN TWENTY-FOUR HOURS."

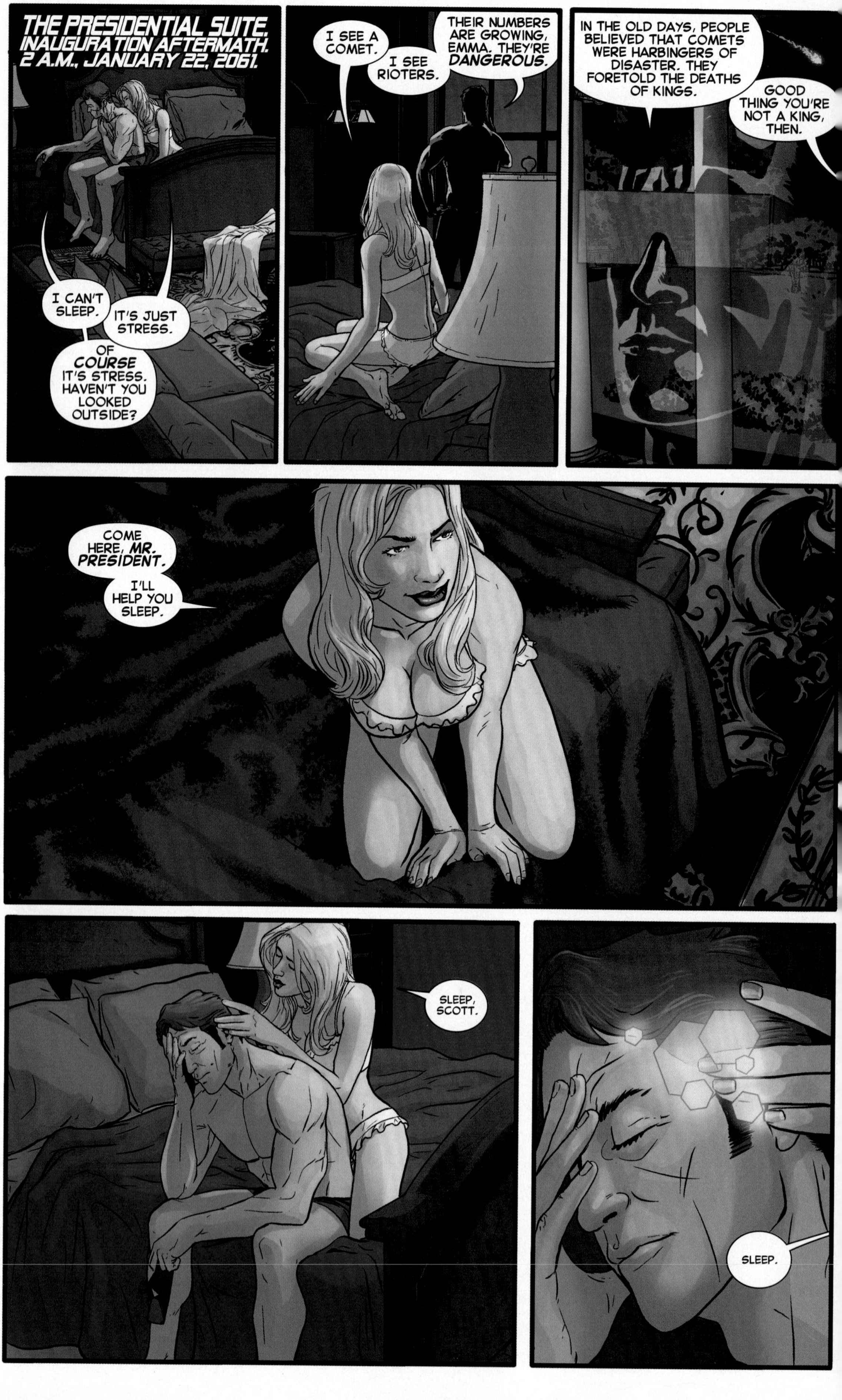
THE PRESIDENTIAL SUITE. INAUGURATION AFTERMATH. 2 A.M., JANUARY 22, 2061.
I CAN'T SLEEP.
IT'S JUST STRESS.
OF COURSE IT'S STRESS. HAVEN'T YOU LOOKED OUTSIDE?
I SEE A COMET.
I SEE RIOTERS.
THEIR NUMBERS ARE GROWING, EMMA. THEY'RE DANGEROUS.
IN THE OLD DAYS, PEOPLE BELIEVED THAT COMETS WERE HARBINGERS OF DISASTER. THEY FORETOLD THE DEATHS OF KINGS.
GOOD THING YOU'RE NOT A KING, THEN.
COME HERE, MR. PRESIDENT.
I'LL HELP YOU SLEEP.
SLEEP, SCOTT.
SLEEP.

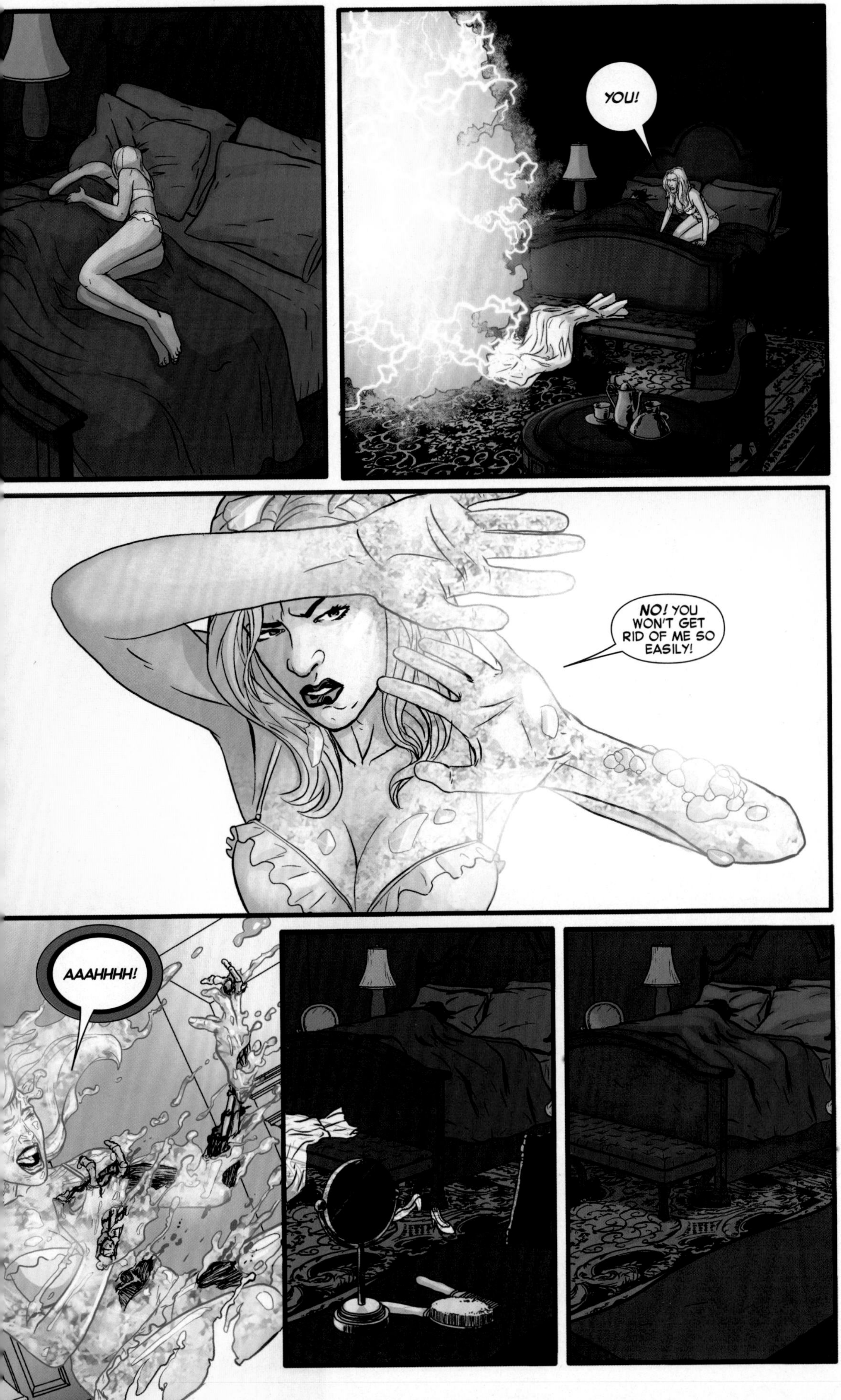
YOU!
NO! YOU WON'T GET RID OF ME SO EASILY!
AAAHHHH!

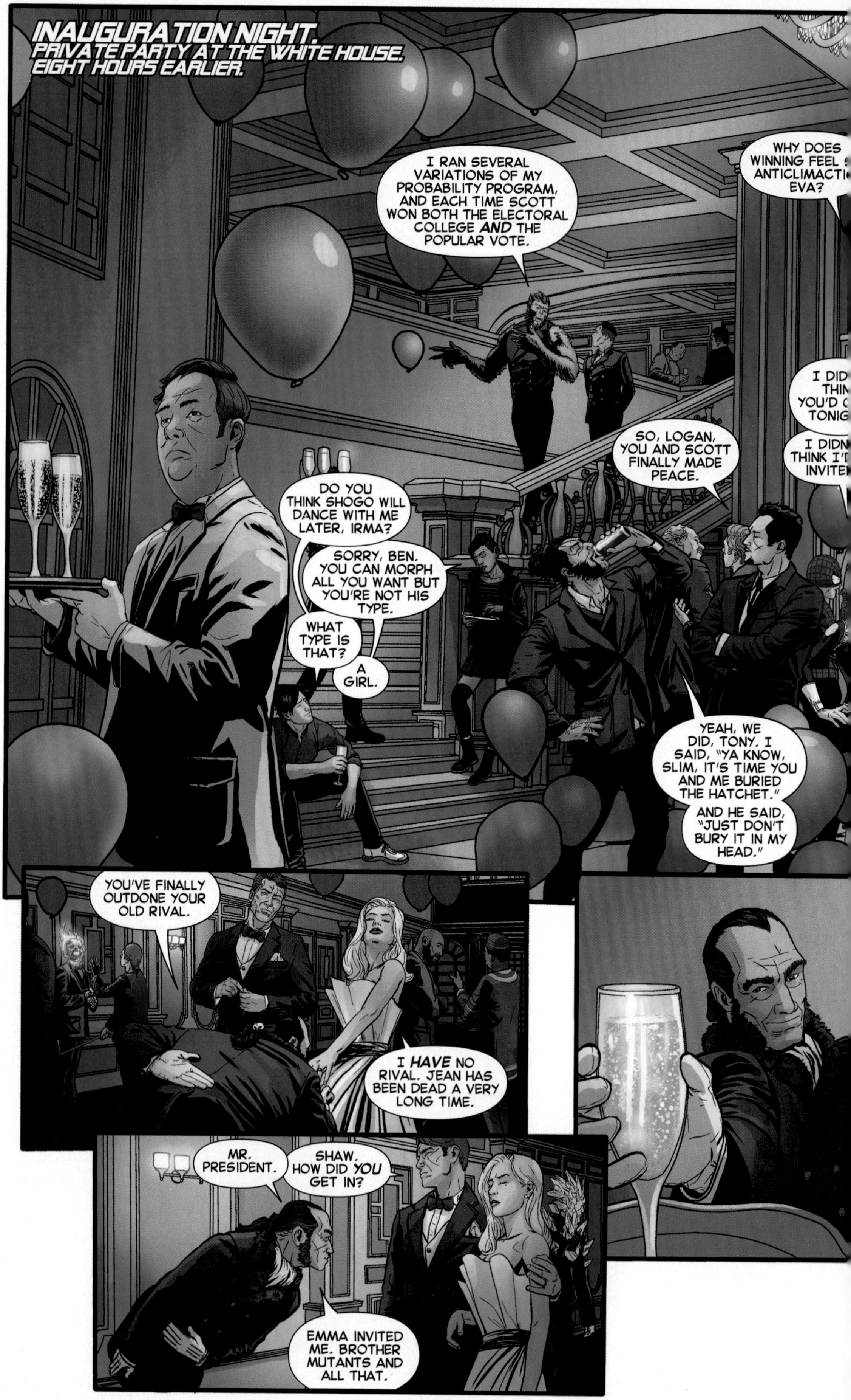
INAUGURATION NIGHT.
PRIVATE PARTY AT THE WHITE HOUSE.
EIGHT HOURS EARLIER.
I RAN SEVERAL VARIATIONS OF MY PROBABILITY PROGRAM, AND EACH TIME SCOTT WON BOTH THE ELECTORAL COLLEGE AND THE POPULAR VOTE.
DO YOU THINK SHOGO WILL DANCE WITH ME LATER, IRMA?
SORRY, BEN. YOU CAN MORPH ALL YOU WANT BUT YOU'RE NOT HIS TYPE.
WHAT TYPE IS THAT?
A GIRL.
SO, LOGAN, YOU AND SCOTT FINALLY MADE PEACE.
YEAH, WE DID, TONY. I SAID, "YA KNOW, SLIM, IT'S TIME YOU AND ME BURIED THE HATCHET."
AND HE SAID, "JUST DON'T BURY IT IN MY HEAD."
YOU'VE FINALLY OUTDONE YOUR OLD RIVAL.
I HAVE NO RIVAL. JEAN HAS BEEN DEAD A VERY LONG TIME.
MR. PRESIDENT.
SHAW. HOW DID YOU GET IN?
EMMA INVITED ME. BROTHER MUTANTS AND ALL THAT.

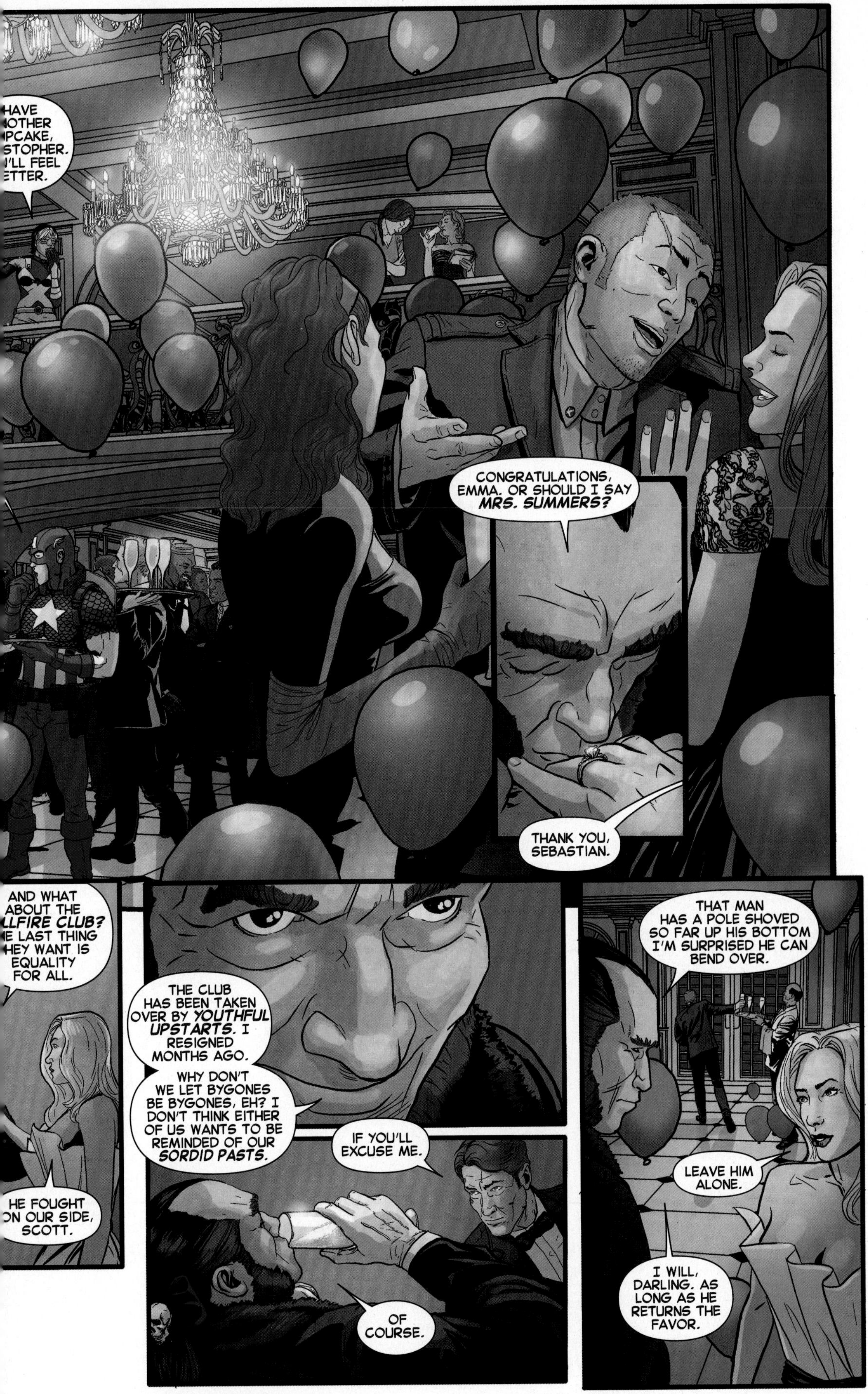
HAVE
NOTHER
PCAKE,
STOPHER.
'LL FEEL
ETTER.
CONGRATULATIONS, EMMA. OR SHOULD I SAY *MRS. SUMMERS?*
THANK YOU, SEBASTIAN.
AND WHAT ABOUT THE *LLFIRE CLUB?* E LAST THING HEY WANT IS EQUALITY FOR ALL.
HE FOUGHT ON OUR SIDE, SCOTT.
THE CLUB HAS BEEN TAKEN OVER BY *YOUTHFUL UPSTARTS.* I RESIGNED MONTHS AGO.
WHY DON'T WE LET BYGONES BE BYGONES, EH? I DON'T THINK EITHER OF US WANTS TO BE REMINDED OF OUR *SORDID PASTS.*
IF YOU'LL EXCUSE ME.
OF COURSE.
THAT MAN HAS A POLE SHOVED SO FAR UP HIS BOTTOM I'M SURPRISED HE CAN BEND OVER.
LEAVE HIM ALONE.
I WILL, DARLING. AS LONG AS HE RETURNS THE FAVOR.

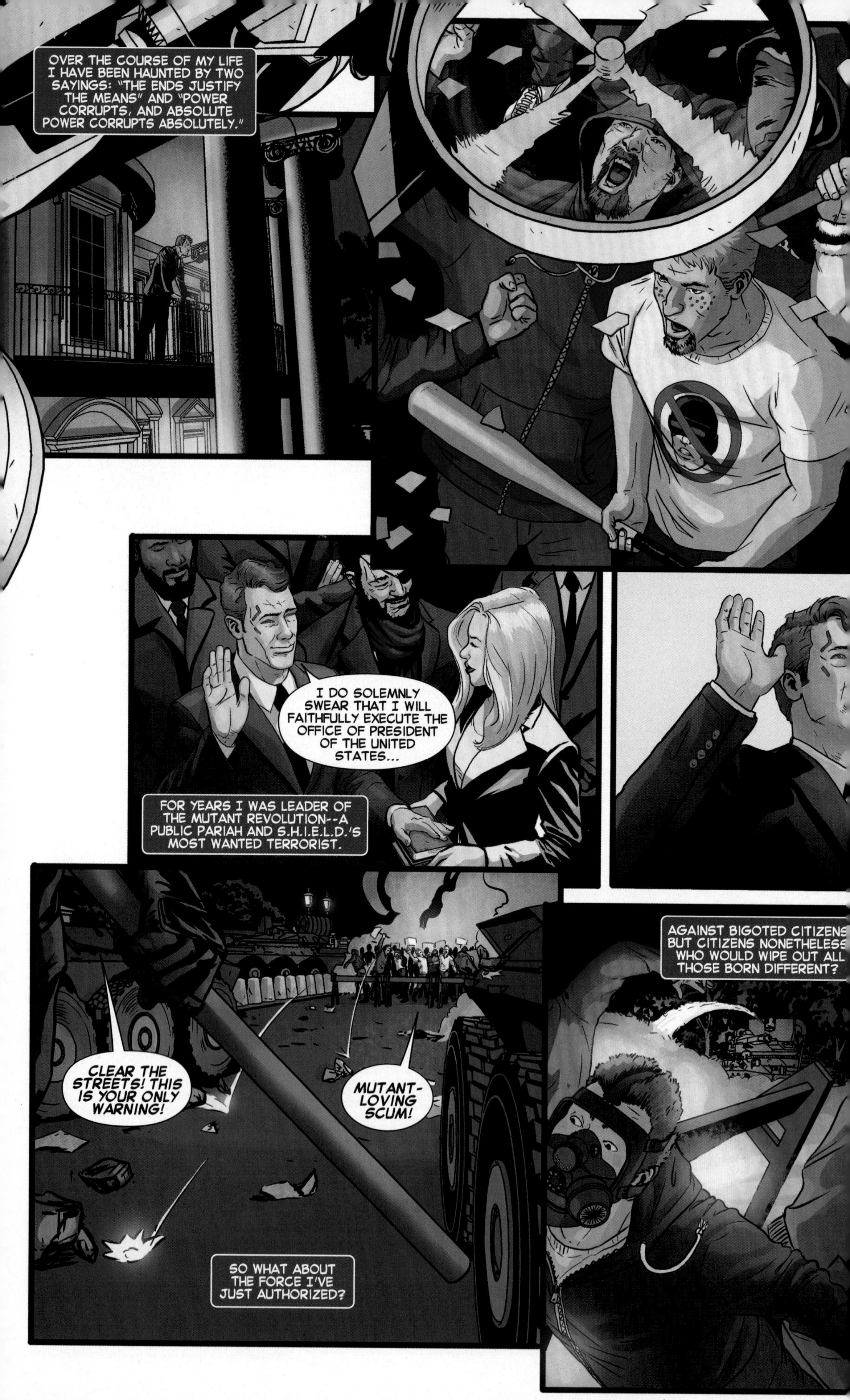
OVER THE COURSE OF MY LIFE I HAVE BEEN HAUNTED BY TWO SAYINGS: "THE ENDS JUSTIFY THE MEANS" AND "POWER CORRUPTS, AND ABSOLUTE POWER CORRUPTS ABSOLUTELY."
I DO SOLEMNLY SWEAR THAT I WILL FAITHFULLY EXECUTE THE OFFICE OF PRESIDENT OF THE UNITED STATES...
FOR YEARS I WAS LEADER OF THE MUTANT REVOLUTION--A PUBLIC PARIAH AND S.H.I.E.L.D.'S MOST WANTED TERRORIST.
CLEAR THE STREETS! THIS IS YOUR ONLY WARNING!
MUTANT-LOVING SCUM!
SO WHAT ABOUT THE FORCE I'VE JUST AUTHORIZED?
AGAINST BIGOTED CITIZENS BUT CITIZENS NONETHELESS WHO WOULD WIPE OUT ALL THOSE BORN DIFFERENT?

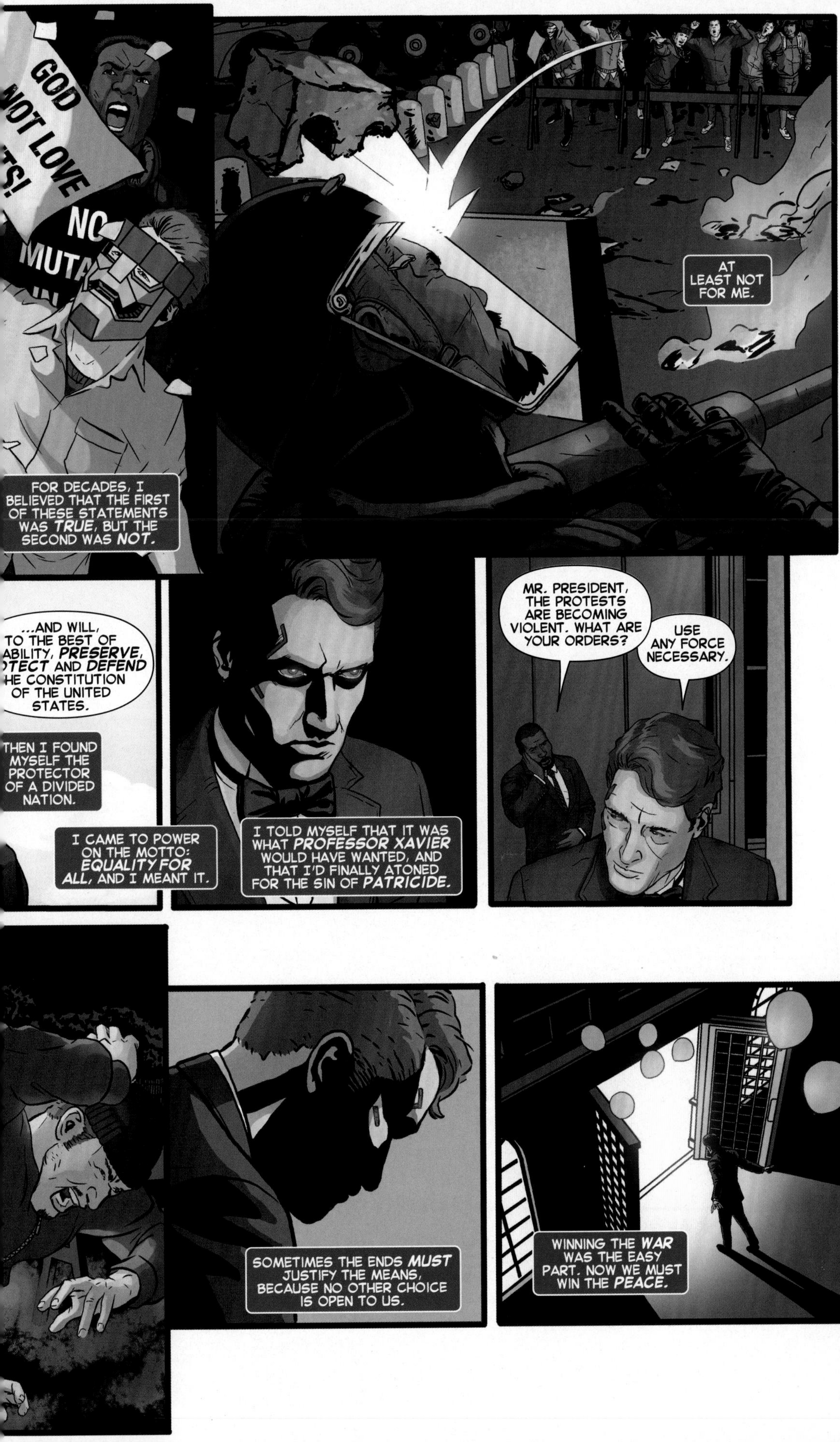
GOD
NOT LOVE
TS!
NO
MUTA
FOR DECADES, I BELIEVED THAT THE FIRST OF THESE STATEMENTS WAS TRUE, BUT THE SECOND WAS NOT.
AT LEAST NOT FOR ME.
...AND WILL, TO THE BEST OF ABILITY, PRESERVE, OTECT AND DEFEND HE CONSTITUTION OF THE UNITED STATES.
THEN I FOUND MYSELF THE PROTECTOR OF A DIVIDED NATION.
I CAME TO POWER ON THE MOTTO: EQUALITY FOR ALL, AND I MEANT IT.
I TOLD MYSELF THAT IT WAS WHAT PROFESSOR XAVIER WOULD HAVE WANTED, AND THAT I'D FINALLY ATONED FOR THE SIN OF PATRICIDE.
MR. PRESIDENT, THE PROTESTS ARE BECOMING VIOLENT. WHAT ARE YOUR ORDERS?
USE ANY FORCE NECESSARY.
SOMETIMES THE ENDS MUST JUSTIFY THE MEANS, BECAUSE NO OTHER CHOICE IS OPEN TO US.
WINNING THE WAR WAS THE EASY PART. NOW WE MUST WIN THE PEACE.

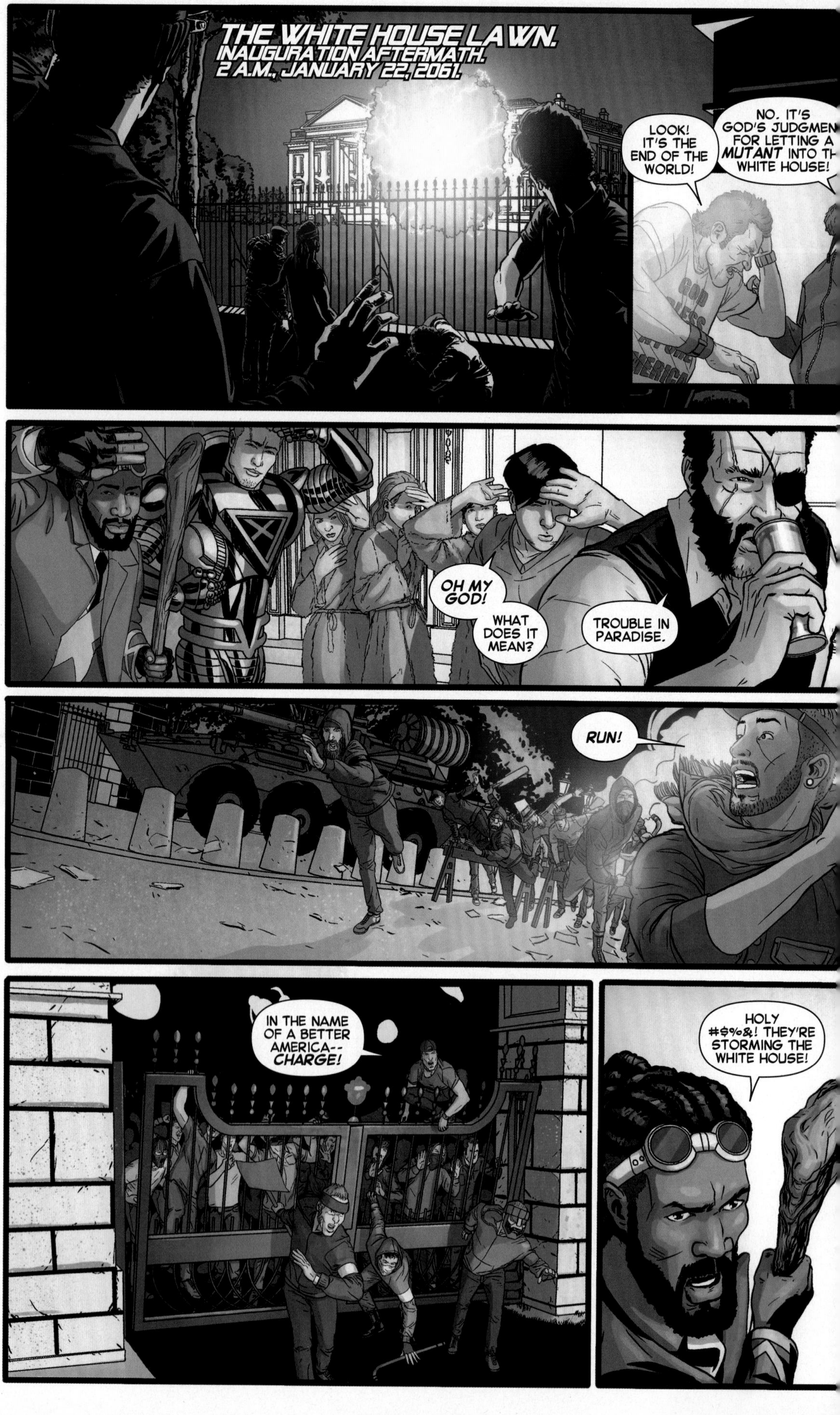
THE WHITE HOUSE LAWN.
INAUGURATION AFTERMATH.
2 A.M., JANUARY 22, 2061.
LOOK! IT'S THE END OF THE WORLD!
NO. IT'S GOD'S JUDGMEN FOR LETTING A MUTANT INTO T WHITE HOUSE!
OH MY GOD!
WHAT DOES IT MEAN?
TROUBLE IN PARADISE.
RUN!
IN THE NAME OF A BETTER AMERICA-- CHARGE!
HOLY #$%&! THEY'RE STORMING THE WHITE HOUSE!

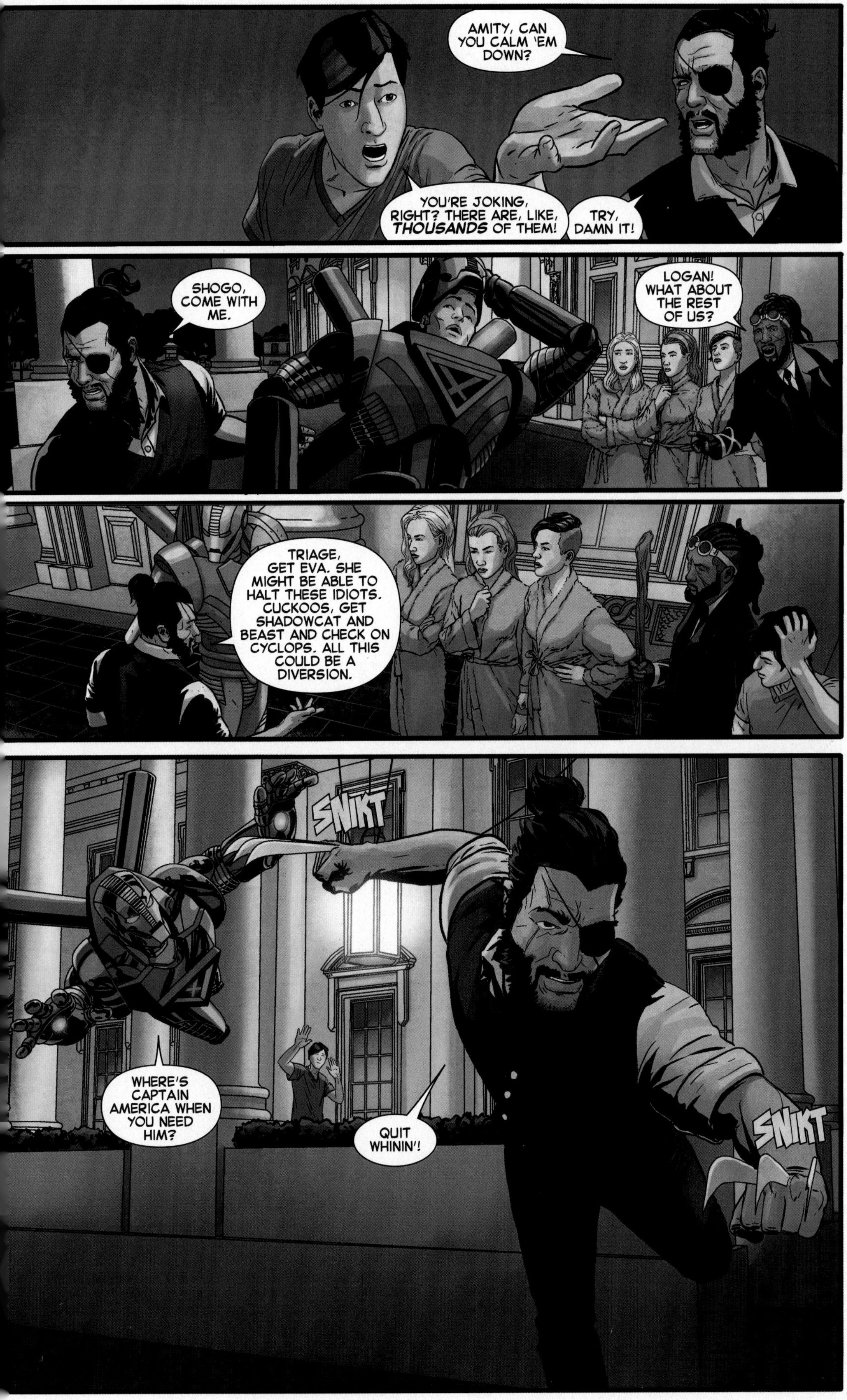
AMITY, CAN YOU CALM 'EM DOWN?
YOU'RE JOKING, RIGHT? THERE ARE, LIKE, *THOUSANDS* OF THEM!
TRY, DAMN IT!
SHOGO, COME WITH ME.
LOGAN! WHAT ABOUT THE REST OF US?
TRIAGE, GET EVA. SHE MIGHT BE ABLE TO HALT THESE IDIOTS. CUCKOOS, GET SHADOWCAT AND BEAST AND CHECK ON CYCLOPS. ALL THIS COULD BE A DIVERSION.
SNIKT
WHERE'S CAPTAIN AMERICA WHEN YOU NEED HIM?
QUIT WHININ'!
SNIKT

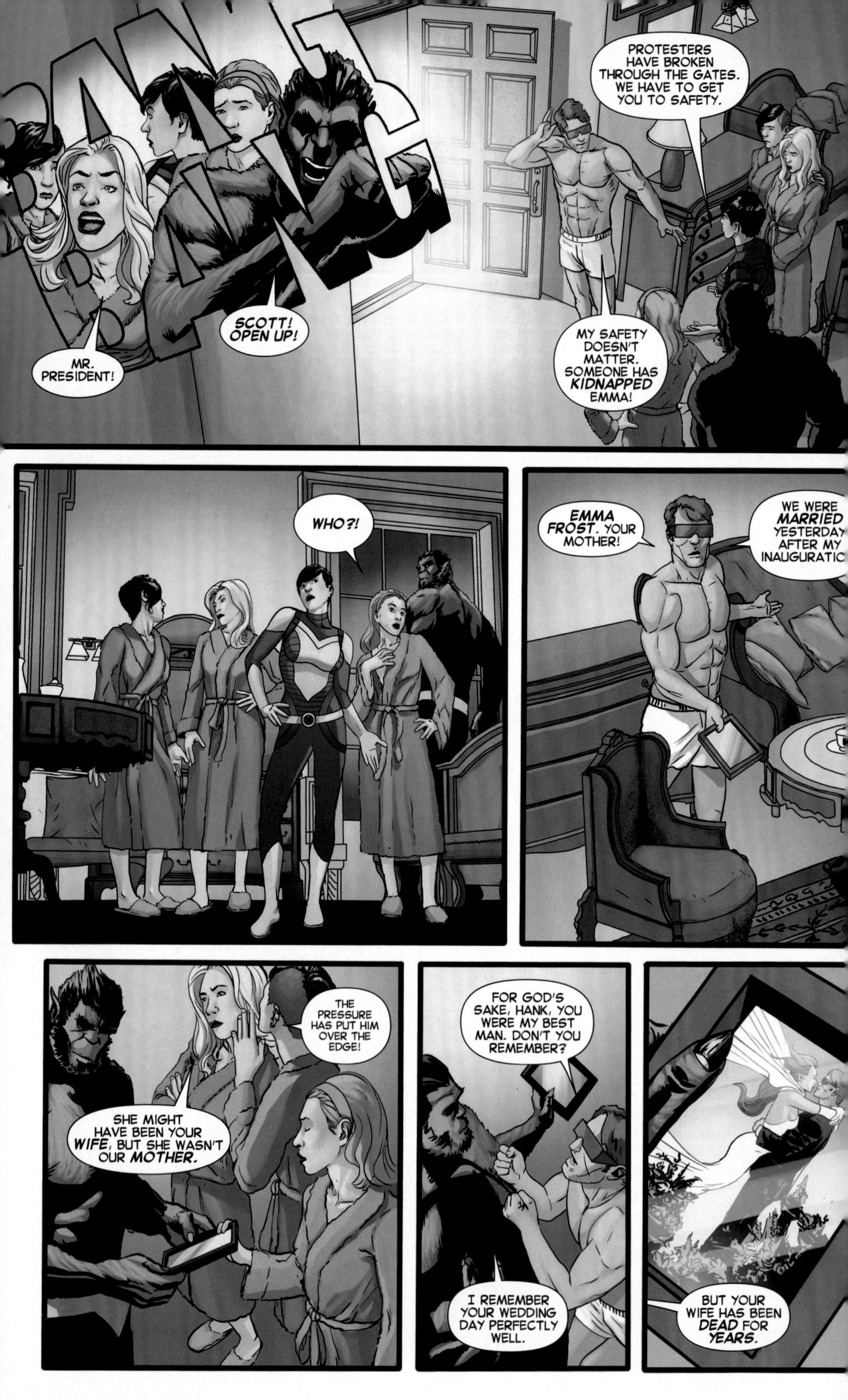
BANG BANG
MR. PRESIDENT!
SCOTT! OPEN UP!
PROTESTERS HAVE BROKEN THROUGH THE GATES. WE HAVE TO GET YOU TO SAFETY.
MY SAFETY DOESN'T MATTER. SOMEONE HAS KIDNAPPED EMMA!
WHO?!
EMMA FROST. YOUR MOTHER!
WE WERE MARRIED YESTERDAY AFTER MY INAUGURATIO
THE PRESSURE HAS PUT HIM OVER THE EDGE!
SHE MIGHT HAVE BEEN YOUR WIFE, BUT SHE WASN'T OUR MOTHER.
FOR GOD'S SAKE, HANK, YOU WERE MY BEST MAN. DON'T YOU REMEMBER?
I REMEMBER YOUR WEDDING DAY PERFECTLY WELL.
BUT YOUR WIFE HAS BEEN DEAD FOR YEARS.

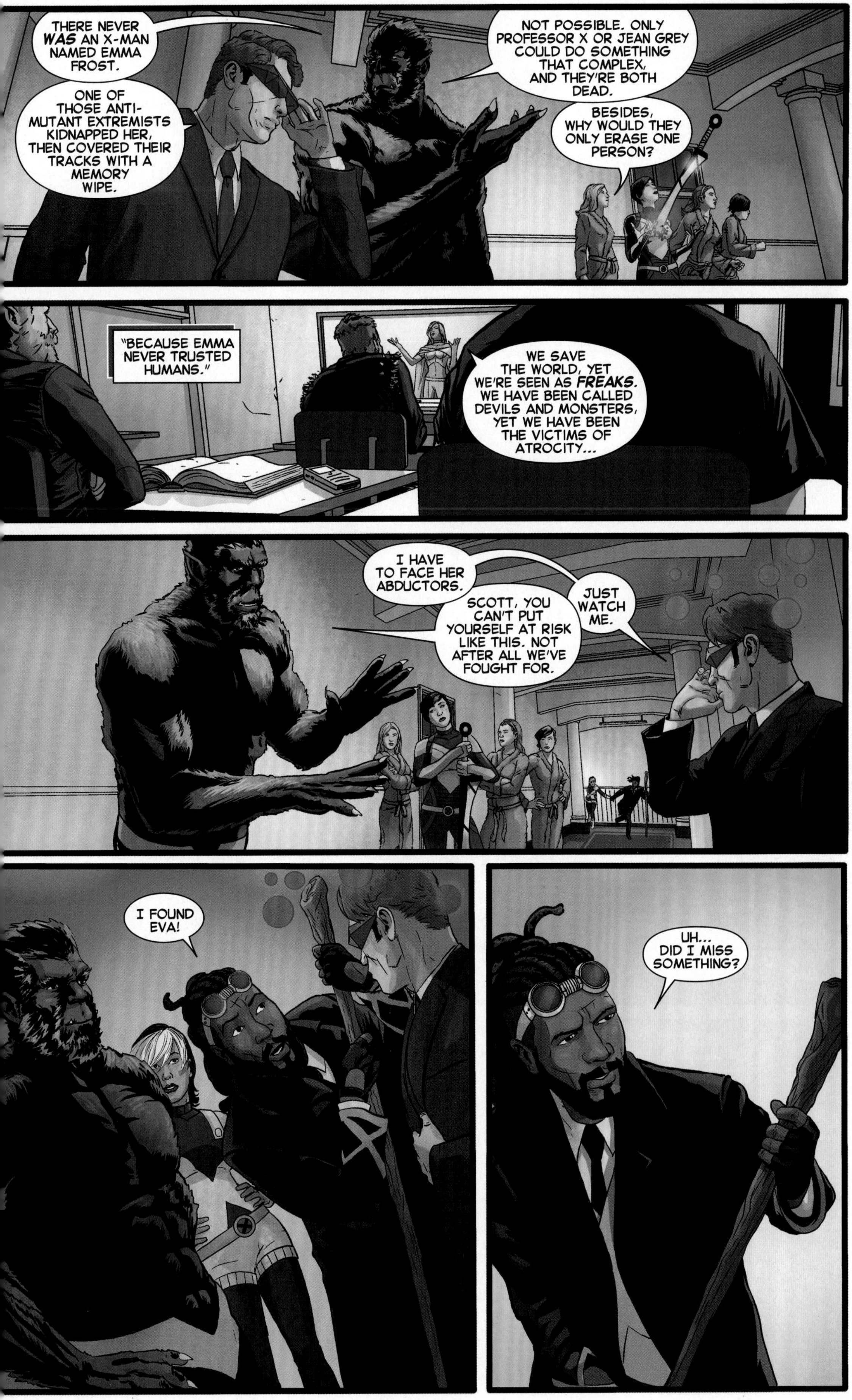
THERE NEVER WAS AN X-MAN NAMED EMMA FROST.
ONE OF THOSE ANTI-MUTANT EXTREMISTS KIDNAPPED HER, THEN COVERED THEIR TRACKS WITH A MEMORY WIPE.
NOT POSSIBLE. ONLY PROFESSOR X OR JEAN GREY COULD DO SOMETHING THAT COMPLEX, AND THEY'RE BOTH DEAD.
BESIDES, WHY WOULD THEY ONLY ERASE ONE PERSON?
"BECAUSE EMMA NEVER TRUSTED HUMANS."
WE SAVE THE WORLD, YET WE'RE SEEN AS FREAKS. WE HAVE BEEN CALLED DEVILS AND MONSTERS, YET WE HAVE BEEN THE VICTIMS OF ATROCITY...
I HAVE TO FACE HER ABDUCTORS.
SCOTT, YOU CAN'T PUT YOURSELF AT RISK LIKE THIS. NOT AFTER ALL WE'VE FOUGHT FOR.
JUST WATCH ME.
I FOUND EVA!
UH... DID I MISS SOMETHING?

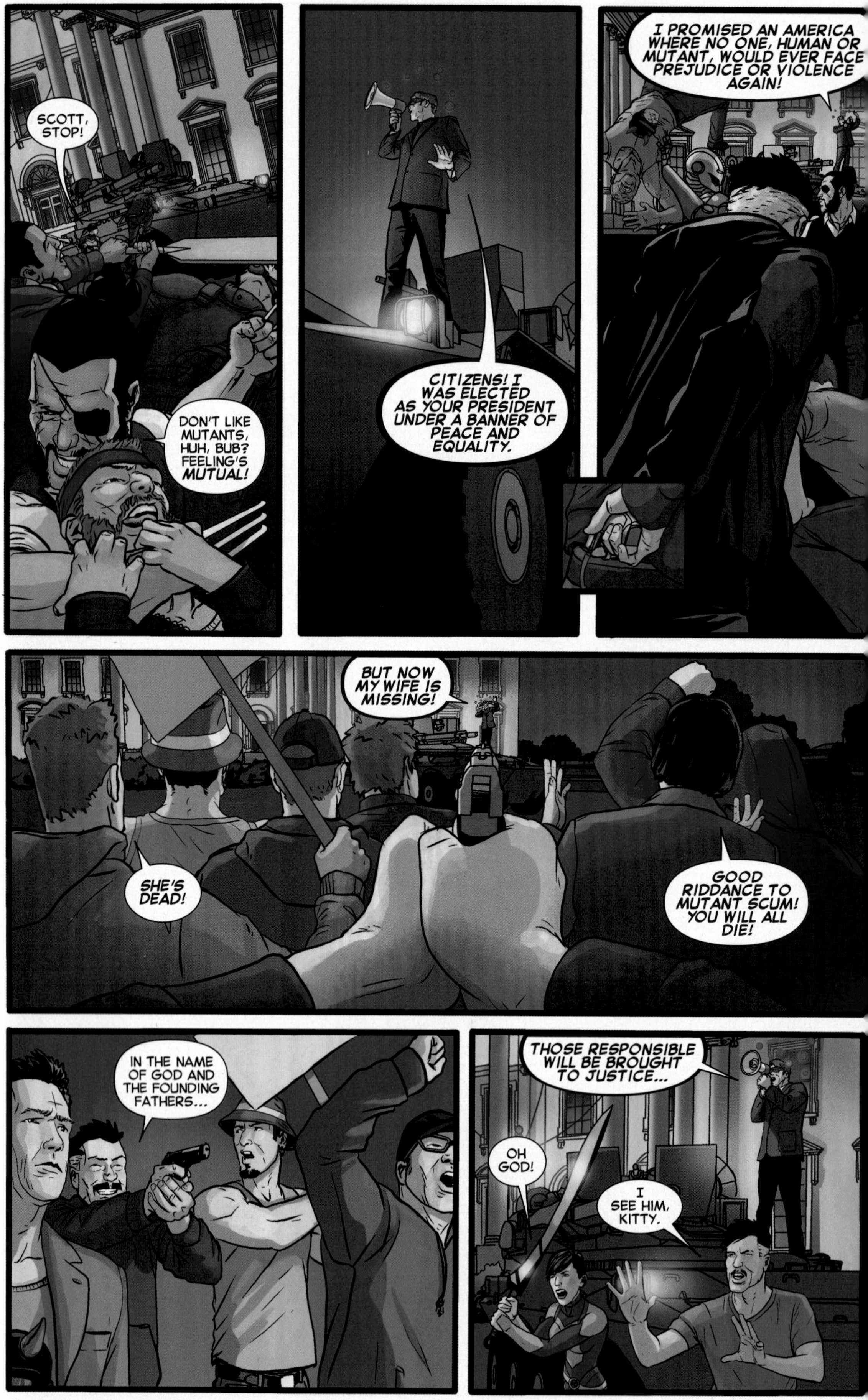
SCOTT, STOP!
DON'T LIKE MUTANTS, HUH, BUB? FEELING'S MUTUAL!
CITIZENS! I WAS ELECTED AS YOUR PRESIDENT UNDER A BANNER OF PEACE AND EQUALITY.
I PROMISED AN AMERICA WHERE NO ONE, HUMAN OR MUTANT, WOULD EVER FACE PREJUDICE OR VIOLENCE AGAIN!
BUT NOW MY WIFE IS MISSING!
SHE'S DEAD!
GOOD RIDDANCE TO MUTANT SCUM! YOU WILL ALL DIE!
IN THE NAME OF GOD AND THE FOUNDING FATHERS...
THOSE RESPONSIBLE WILL BE BROUGHT TO JUSTICE...
OH GOD!
I SEE HIM, KITTY.

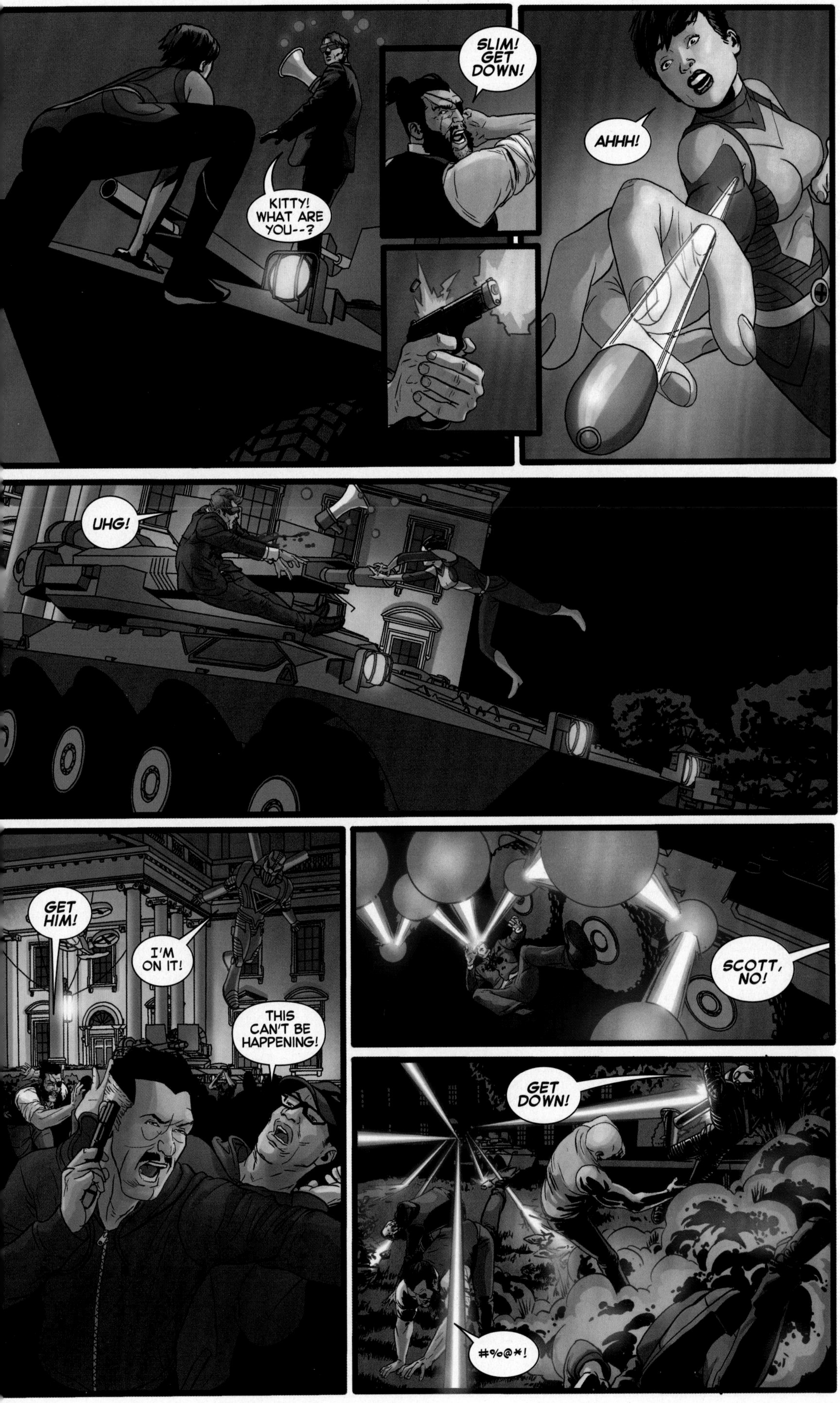
KITTY! WHAT ARE YOU--?
SLIM! GET DOWN!
AHHH!
UHG!
GET HIM!
I'M ON IT!
THIS CAN'T BE HAPPENING!
SCOTT, NO!
GET DOWN!
#%@*!

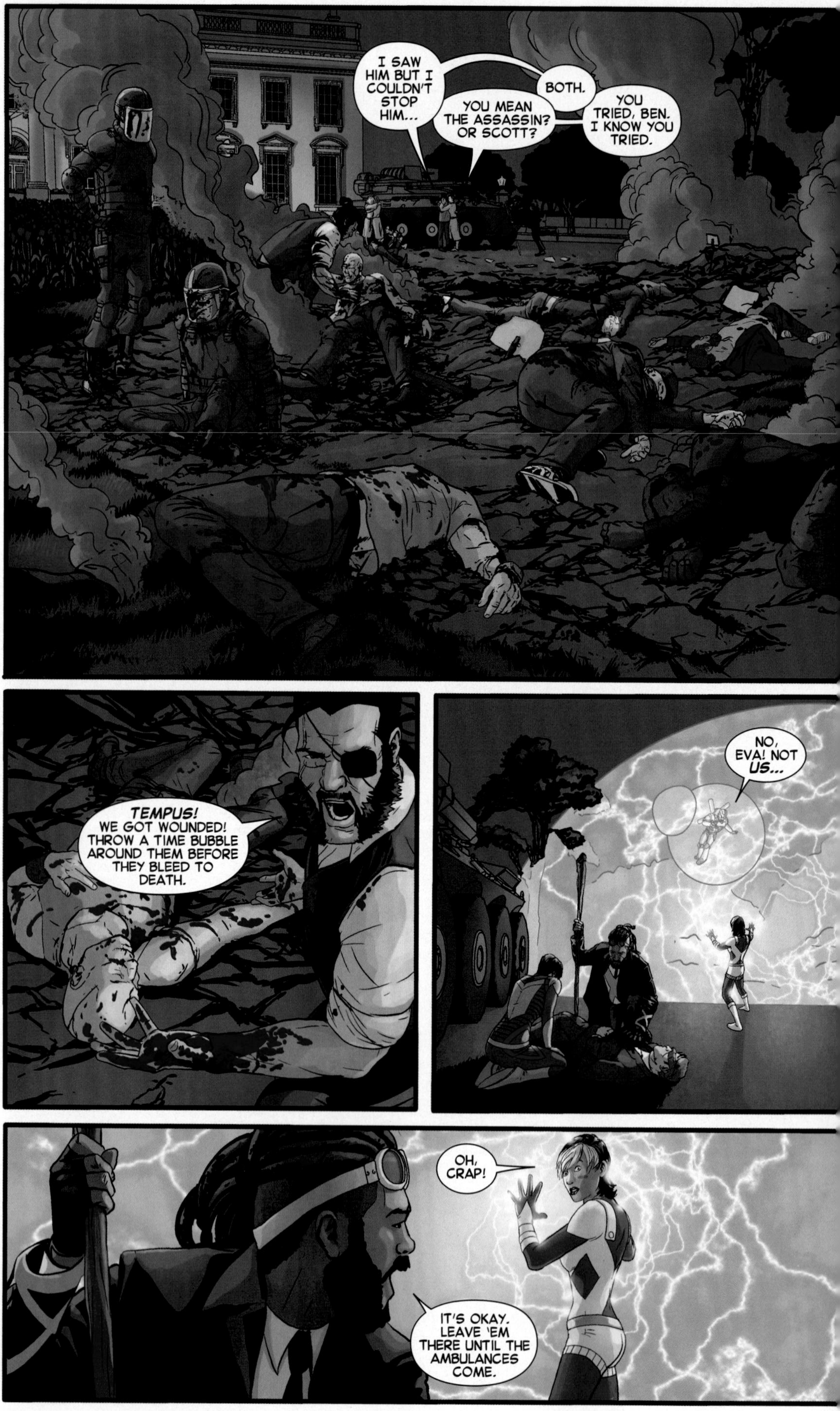
I SAW HIM BUT I COULDN'T STOP HIM...
YOU MEAN THE ASSASSIN? OR SCOTT?
BOTH.
YOU TRIED, BEN. I KNOW YOU TRIED.
TEMPUS! WE GOT WOUNDED! THROW A TIME BUBBLE AROUND THEM BEFORE THEY BLEED TO DEATH.
NO, EVA! NOT *US...*
OH, CRAP!
IT'S OKAY. LEAVE 'EM THERE UNTIL THE AMBULANCES COME.

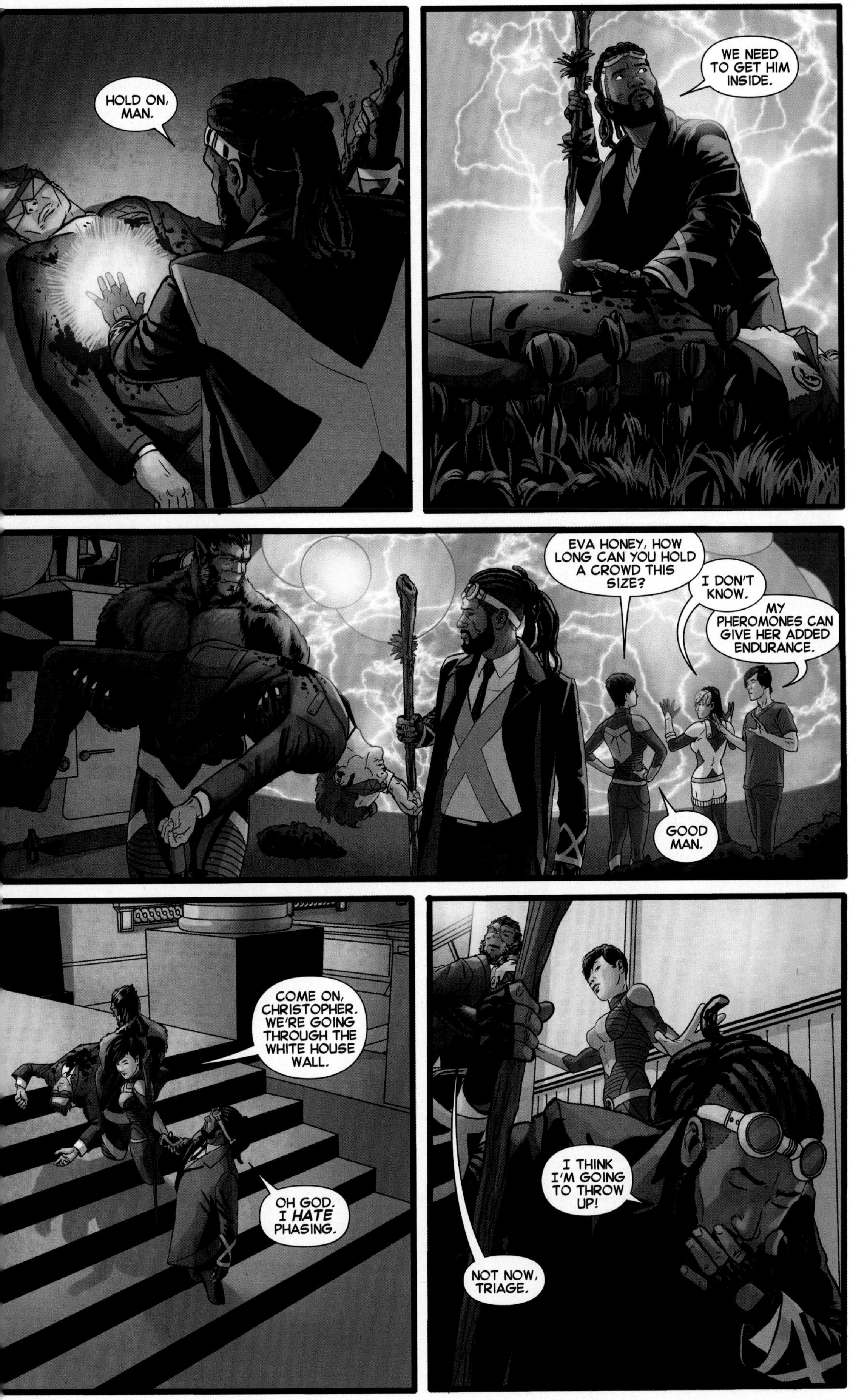

HOLD ON, MAN.
WE NEED TO GET HIM INSIDE.
EVA HONEY, HOW LONG CAN YOU HOLD A CROWD THIS SIZE?
I DON'T KNOW.
MY PHEROMONES CAN GIVE HER ADDED ENDURANCE.
GOOD MAN.
COME ON, CHRISTOPHER. WE'RE GOING THROUGH THE WHITE HOUSE WALL.
OH GOD. I *HATE* PHASING.
I THINK I'M GOING TO THROW UP!
NOT NOW, TRIAGE.

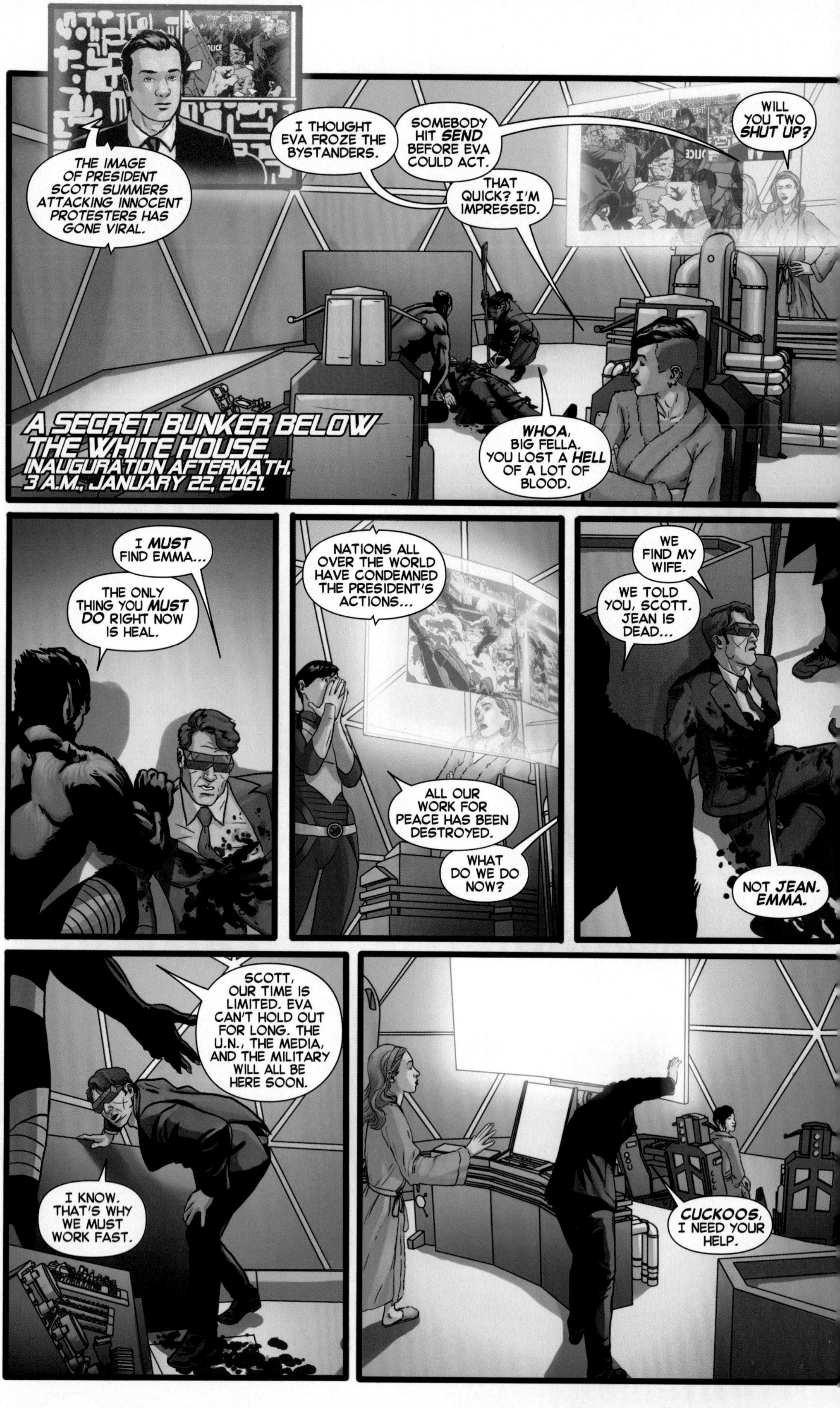
THE IMAGE OF PRESIDENT SCOTT SUMMERS ATTACKING INNOCENT PROTESTERS HAS GONE VIRAL.
I THOUGHT EVA FROZE THE BYSTANDERS.
SOMEBODY HIT SEND BEFORE EVA COULD ACT.
THAT QUICK? I'M IMPRESSED.
WILL YOU TWO SHUT UP?
A SECRET BUNKER BELOW THE WHITE HOUSE. INAUGURATION AFTERMATH. 3 A.M., JANUARY 22, 2061.
WHOA, BIG FELLA. YOU LOST A HELL OF A LOT OF BLOOD.
I MUST FIND EMMA...
THE ONLY THING YOU MUST DO RIGHT NOW IS HEAL.
NATIONS ALL OVER THE WORLD HAVE CONDEMNED THE PRESIDENT'S ACTIONS...
ALL OUR WORK FOR PEACE HAS BEEN DESTROYED.
WHAT DO WE DO NOW?
WE FIND MY WIFE.
WE TOLD YOU, SCOTT. JEAN IS DEAD...
NOT JEAN. EMMA.
SCOTT, OUR TIME IS LIMITED. EVA CAN'T HOLD OUT FOR LONG. THE U.N., THE MEDIA, AND THE MILITARY WILL ALL BE HERE SOON.
I KNOW. THAT'S WHY WE MUST WORK FAST.
CUCKOOS, I NEED YOUR HELP.

WHAT ARE WE SEARCHING FOR?

AN *OMEGA-CLASS* TELEPATH WITHIN A HUNDRED MILE RADIUS OF THE WHITE HOUSE.

SOMEONE POWERFUL ENOUGH TO CREATE A MEMORY WIPE COULD ALSO BLOCK CEREBRO.

CRASH

THERE *MUST* BE ANOTHER WAY.

THERE *IS.* PROFESSOR X'S *LOCKBOX PROGRAM.*

BRILLIANT!

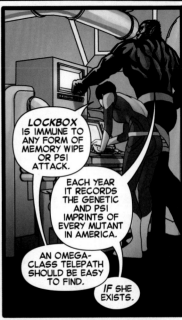

LOCKBOX IS IMMUNE TO ANY FORM OF MEMORY WIPE OR PSI ATTACK.

EACH YEAR IT RECORDS THE GENETIC AND PSI IMPRINTS OF EVERY MUTANT IN AMERICA.

AN OMEGA-CLASS TELEPATH SHOULD BE EASY TO FIND.

IF SHE EXISTS.

SCOTT, WHERE DID THIS "EMMA" RESIDE BEFORE COMING TO THE WHITE HOUSE WITH YOU?

THE WEAPON X COMPOUND IN ALBERTA, CANADA.

OH, MY STARS AND GARTERS. I THINK WE FOUND HER.

GIRLS, CAN YOU TAKE A READING OF THE NATION'S PRESENT COLLECTIVE MUTANT PSI FORCE?

PUT THE MUTANTS IN GREEN. I WANT TO DO A COMPARISON WITH THE GENERAL POPULATION.

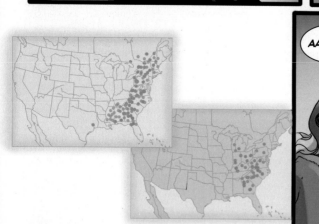

AAAHHH!

DAMN!

SCOTT, IT'S NOT JUST THIS MYSTERIOUS EMMA WHO HAS DISAPPEARED.

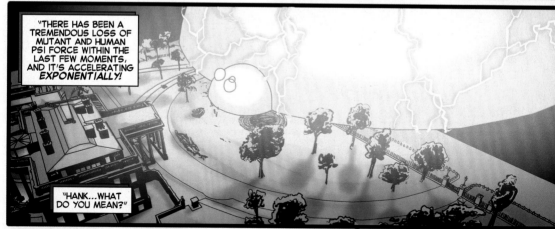

"THERE HAS BEEN A TREMENDOUS LOSS OF MUTANT AND HUMAN PSI FORCE WITHIN THE LAST FEW MOMENTS, AND IT'S ACCELERATING EXPONENTIALLY!"

"HANK...WHAT DO YOU MEAN?"

THEY'RE... THEY'RE JUST BLINKING OUT OF EXISTENCE!

AAAHHHH!

HANK!

HANK? KITTY? CHRISTOPHER? GIRLS? ARE YOU HERE?

NO, SCOTT. NOT ANYMORE.

WHAT HAVE YOU DONE TO EMMA? AND TO THE OTHERS?

REMOVED THEM FROM THE TIME/SPACE CONTINUUM. TECHNICALLY THEY HAVE NEVER EXISTED.

THE WHITE HOT ROOM.
HEART OF THE PHOENIX.

BUT I *REMEMBER* THEM.

YES.

JEAN. I SHOULD HAVE KNOWN.

BUT YOU'RE *NOT* JEAN, ARE YOU? YOU'RE CHAOS-BRINGER. STARCHILDE. *DARK PHOENIX.*

NO, SCOTT. JUST *PHOENIX.*

DARK PHOENIX IS BORN OF HUMAN DESIRE. AND I AM THE EMBODIMENT OF ETERNITY.

HAVE YOU COME TO RUIN MY LIFE AGAIN?

WHY NOW, WHEN I HAVE ATONED FOR SO MUCH?

THE WORLD IS NOT READY FOR YOU TO LEAD IT.

YOUR PRESIDENCY WILL BRING ABOUT *WAR* AND *DISASTER.*

NO!

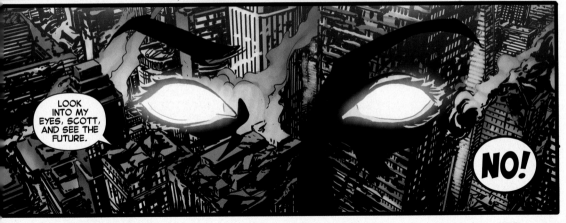

LOOK INTO MY EYES, SCOTT, AND SEE THE FUTURE.

NO!

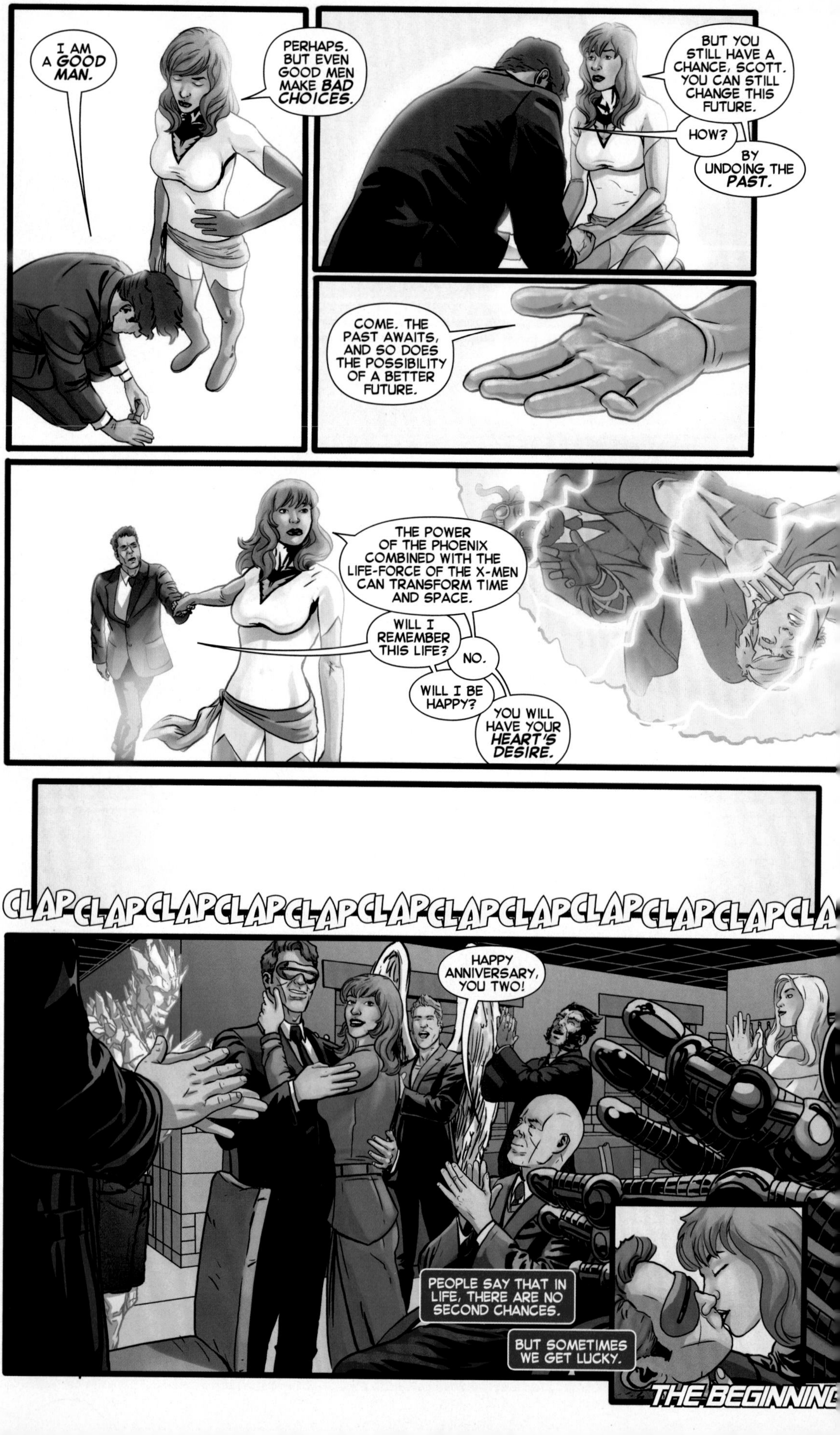
I AM A GOOD MAN.
PERHAPS. BUT EVEN GOOD MEN MAKE BAD CHOICES.
BUT YOU STILL HAVE A CHANCE, SCOTT. YOU CAN STILL CHANGE THIS FUTURE.
HOW?
BY UNDOING THE PAST.
COME. THE PAST AWAITS, AND SO DOES THE POSSIBILITY OF A BETTER FUTURE.
THE POWER OF THE PHOENIX COMBINED WITH THE LIFE-FORCE OF THE X-MEN CAN TRANSFORM TIME AND SPACE.
WILL I REMEMBER THIS LIFE?
NO.
WILL I BE HAPPY?
YOU WILL HAVE YOUR HEART'S DESIRE.
CLAPCLAPCLAPCLAPCLAPCLAPCLAPCLAPCLAPCLAPCLAPCLA
HAPPY ANNIVERSARY, YOU TWO!
PEOPLE SAY THAT IN LIFE, THERE ARE NO SECOND CHANCES.
BUT SOMETIMES WE GET LUCKY.
THE BEGINNIN

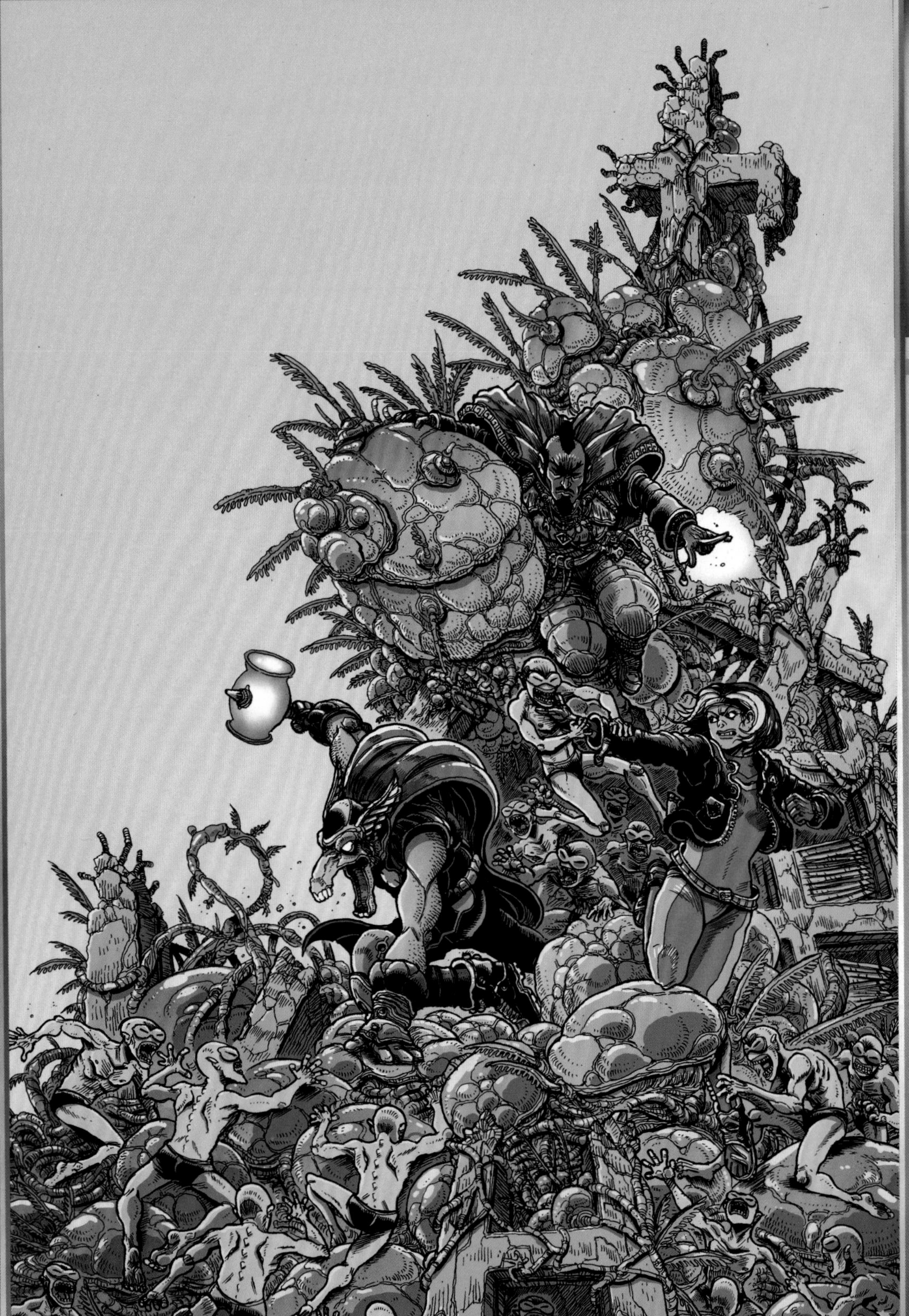

100TH ANNIVERSARY SPECIAL: AVENGERS

JAMES STOKOE
story, art and cover

ALEXANDER LOZANO
variant cover

JON MOISAN
editor

THE AVENGERS

CONSOLIDATING AFTER THE BRUTAL *SEVENTH GENDER WAR*, THE *BADOON EMPIRE* FINDS ITSELF STRONGER THAN EVER. RAPIDLY EXPANDING OUTWARD ALONG THE GALACTIC SPIRAL, THEIR ARMADA FINALLY FINDS ITSELF AT *EARTH'S* DOORSTEP.

THE AVENGERS; EARTH'S MIGHTIEST HEROES, HEED THE CALL TO ACTION AND FIGHT OFF WAVE AFTER WAVE OF THE SEEMINGLY ENDLESS BADOON. FINALLY, WITH THE SUDDEN INTERVENTION OF *DR. FRANKLIN RICHARDS: HERALD OF GALACTUS,* THE BADOON ARE THROWN BACK INTO THE DEPTHS OF SPACE TO LICK THEIR WOUNDS.

BUT THE WAR HAS COST THE EARTH DEARLY. A GREAT FLOOD OF *BIO-SPORES* LITTER THE GLOBE, SLOWLY POISONING ITS ATMOSPHERE. PERHAPS MOST DEVASTATING WAS THE GREAT *TERROR WEAPON* LAUNCHED IN THE OPENING STAGES OF THE INVASION, TRANSPORTING THE ENTIRE *AMERICAN CONTINENT* INTO THE STRANGE AND UNKNOWABLE *NEGATIVE ZONE.*

NOW, WITH MOST OF ITS MEMBERS SCATTERED, THE FEW REMAINING *AVENGERS* REGROUP AT THEIR HOME BASE IN *MALAYSIA,* WHILE A GRIEF STRICKEN *CAPTAIN AMERICA* EMBARKS ON A ONE-MAN ODYSSEY INTO THE *NEGATIVE ZONE* TO FIND HIS LOST HOMELAND...

GONE BUT NOT FORGOTTEN
JAMES STOKOE 1985-2063
AS YOU MAY HAVE HEARD, OUR ARTIST FOR THIS ISSUE, COMICS VETERAN *JAMES STOKOE,* IS NO LONGER WITH US AFTER BEING CLIPPED BY A ROGUE SKYBIKE. WHILE UNABLE TO PERSONALLY FINISH THE BOOK BEFORE HIS UNTIMELY DEATH, WE HAVE EMPLOYED OUR PATENTED *MARVEL BRAIN ALGORITHM* TO DEDUCE WHAT JAMES' LAST FEW PAGES WOULD HAVE LOOKED LIKE. WE APOLOGIZE FOR ANY DISCREPANCIES AND HOPE YOU ENJOY THE ISSUE!

MISS YOU, *JIMMY!*

AXEL ALONSO - editor in chief

JOE QUESADA - chief creative office

DAN BUCKLEY - publisher

ALAN FINE - executive producer

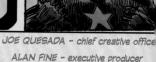
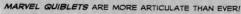

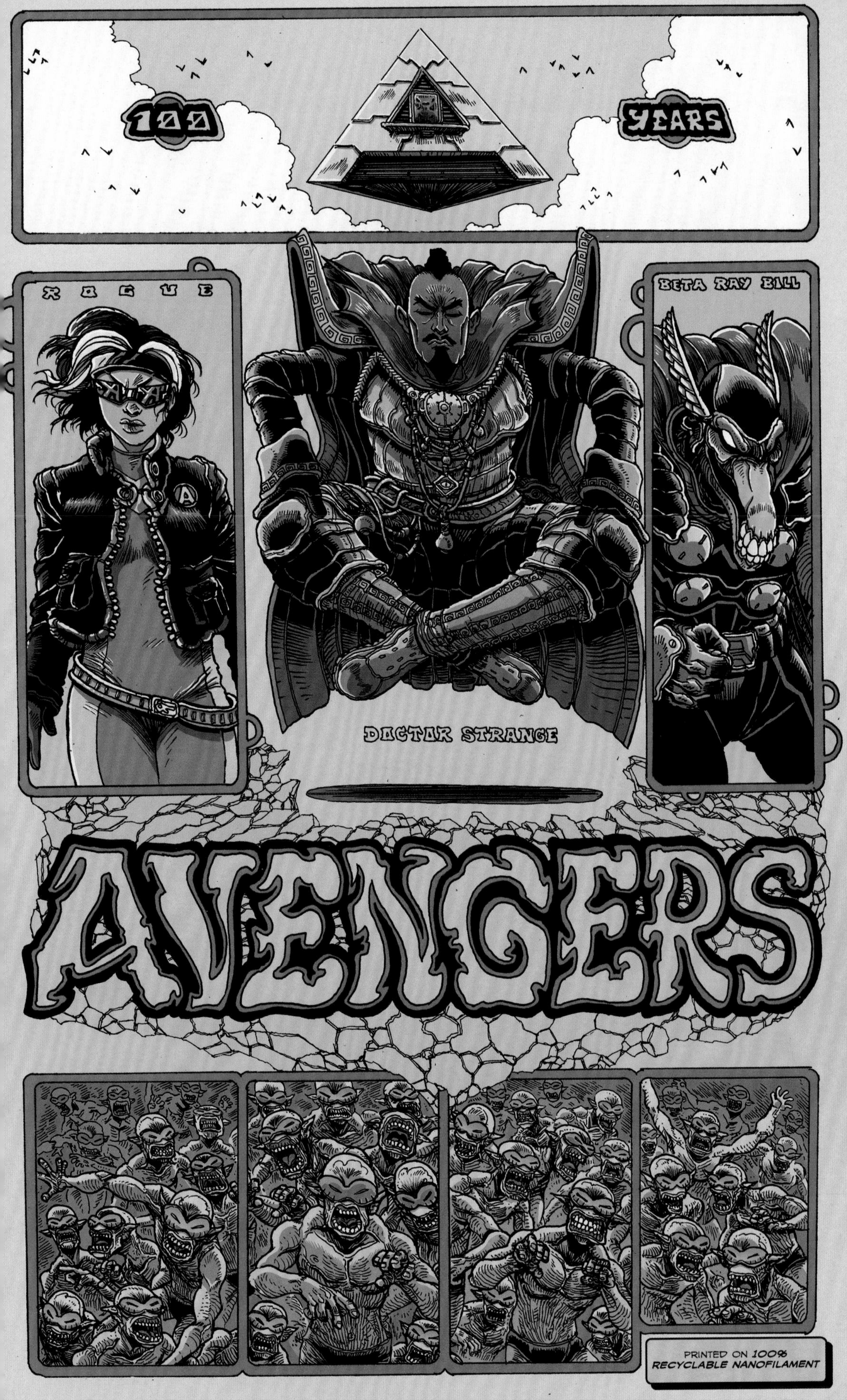

100
YEARS
ROGUE
BETA RAY BILL
DOCTOR STRANGE
AVENGERS
PRINTED ON 100%
RECYCLABLE NANOFILAMENT

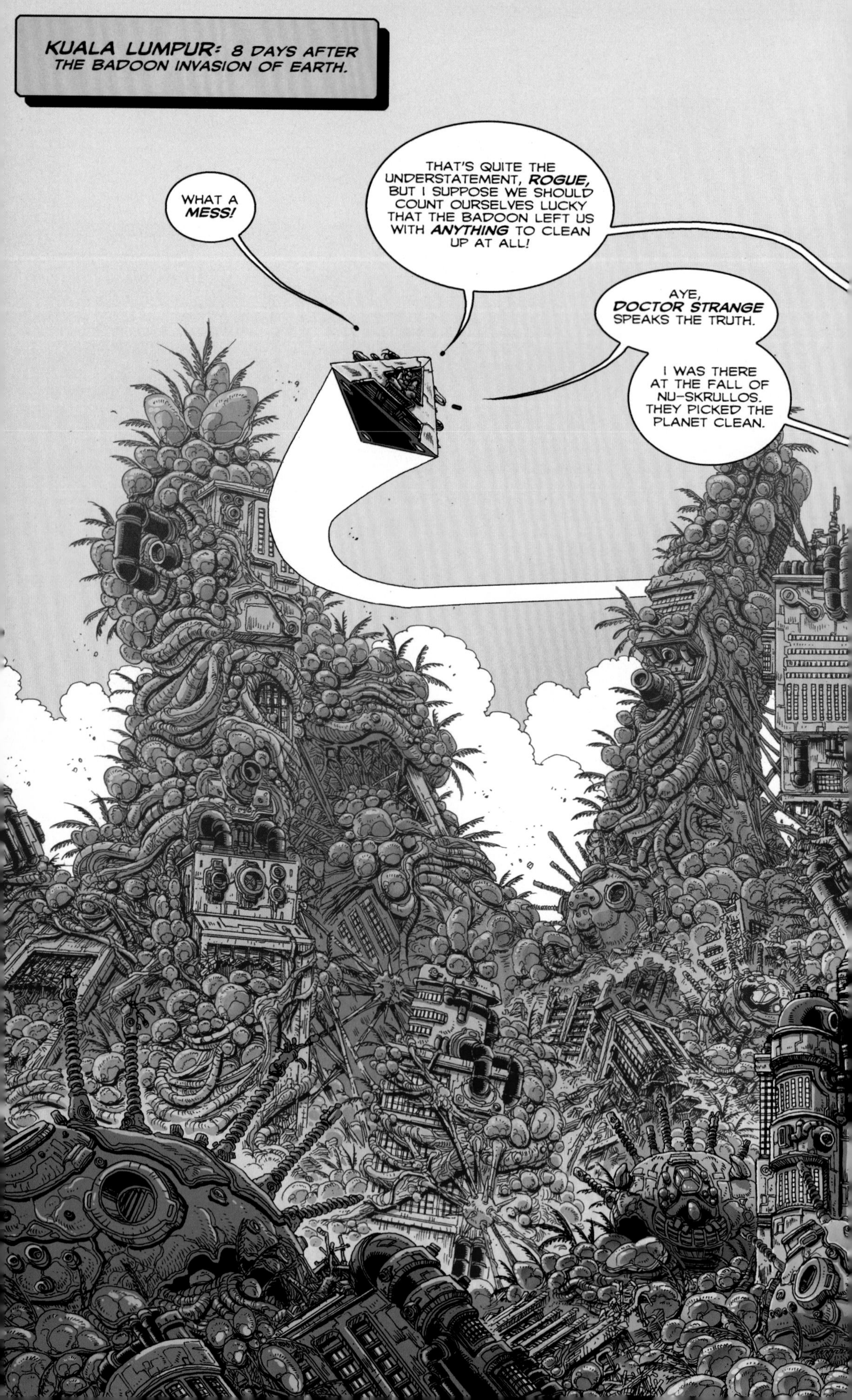
KUALA LUMPUR: 8 DAYS AFTER THE BADOON INVASION OF EARTH.
WHAT A MESS!
THAT'S QUITE THE UNDERSTATEMENT, ROGUE, BUT I SUPPOSE WE SHOULD COUNT OURSELVES LUCKY THAT THE BADOON LEFT US WITH ANYTHING TO CLEAN UP AT ALL!
AYE, DOCTOR STRANGE SPEAKS THE TRUTH.
I WAS THERE AT THE FALL OF NU-SKRULLOS. THEY PICKED THE PLANET CLEAN.

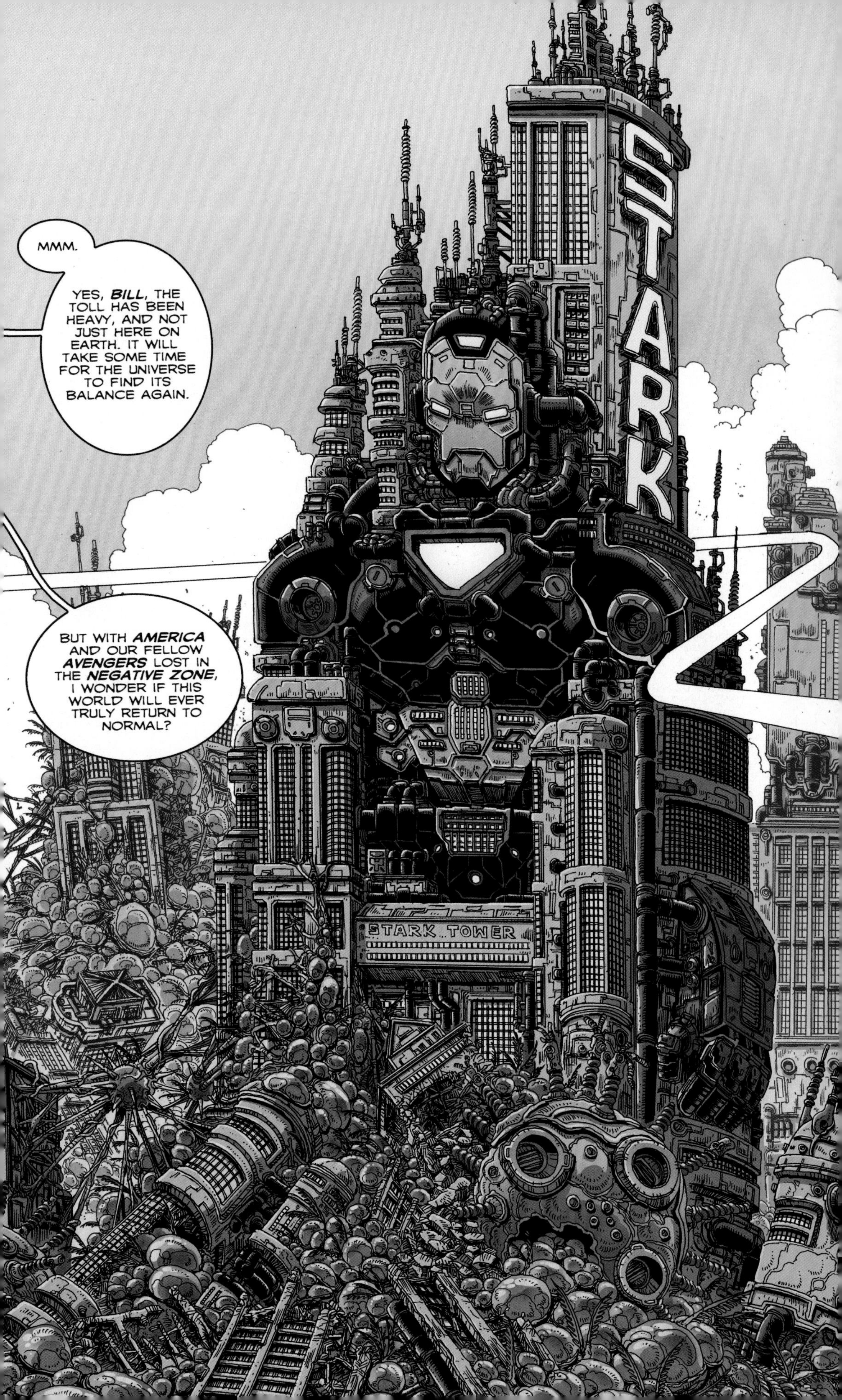
MMM.
YES, BILL, THE TOLL HAS BEEN HEAVY, AND NOT JUST HERE ON EARTH. IT WILL TAKE SOME TIME FOR THE UNIVERSE TO FIND ITS BALANCE AGAIN.
STARK
BUT WITH AMERICA AND OUR FELLOW AVENGERS LOST IN THE NEGATIVE ZONE, I WONDER IF THIS WORLD WILL EVER TRULY RETURN TO NORMAL?
STARK TOWER

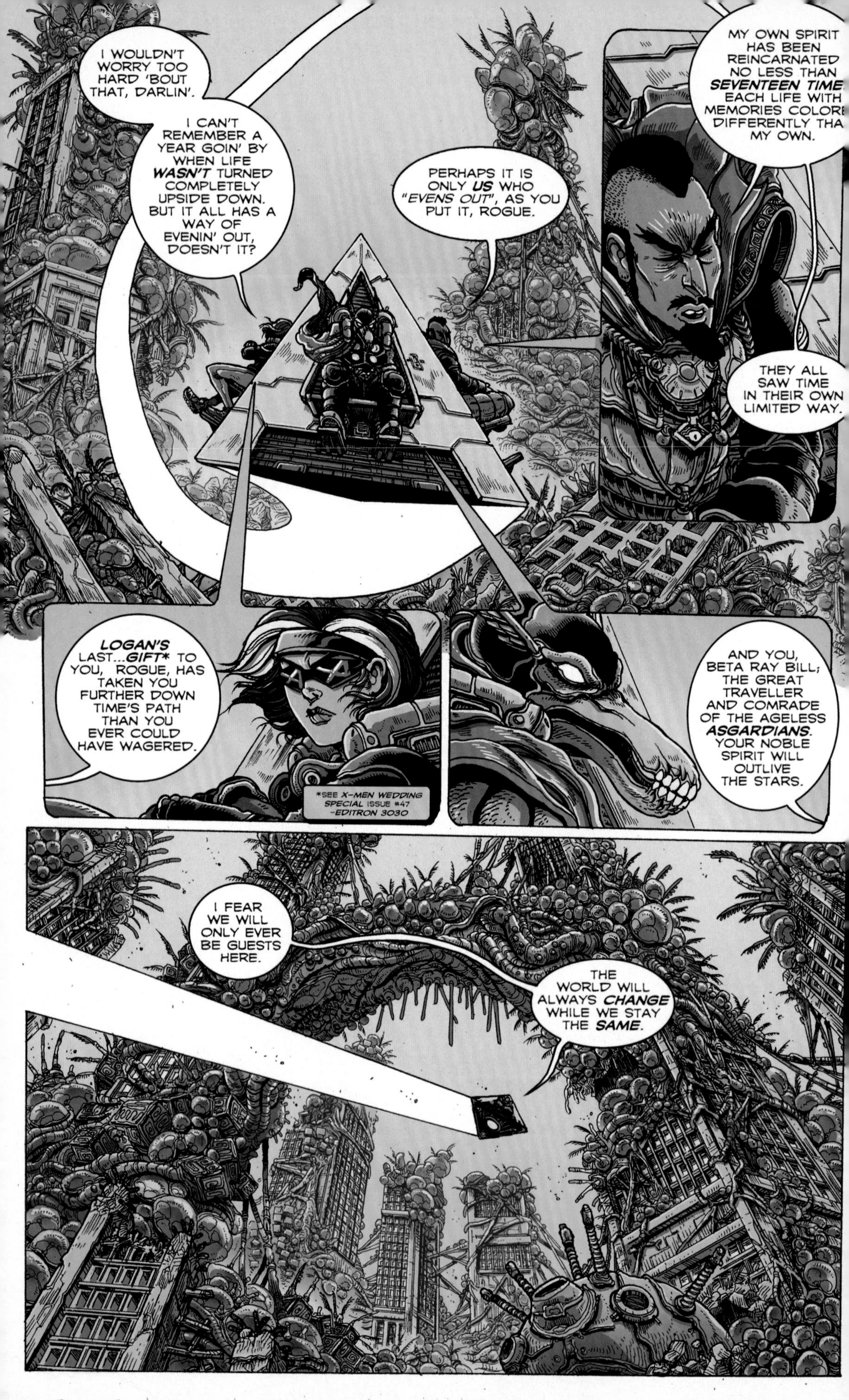

I WOULDN'T WORRY TOO HARD 'BOUT THAT, DARLIN'.
I CAN'T REMEMBER A YEAR GOIN' BY WHEN LIFE *WASN'T* TURNED COMPLETELY UPSIDE DOWN. BUT IT ALL HAS A WAY OF EVENIN' OUT, DOESN'T IT?
PERHAPS IT IS ONLY *US* WHO *"EVENS OUT"*, AS YOU PUT IT, ROGUE.
MY OWN SPIRIT HAS BEEN REINCARNATED NO LESS THAN *SEVENTEEN TIME* EACH LIFE WITH MEMORIES COLORE DIFFERENTLY THA MY OWN.
THEY ALL SAW TIME IN THEIR OWN LIMITED WAY.
LOGAN'S LAST...*GIFT** TO YOU, ROGUE, HAS TAKEN YOU FURTHER DOWN TIME'S PATH THAN YOU EVER COULD HAVE WAGERED.
*SEE *X-MEN WEDDING SPECIAL* ISSUE #47 -EDITRON 3030
AND YOU, BETA RAY BILL; THE GREAT TRAVELLER AND COMRADE OF THE AGELESS *ASGARDIANS*. YOUR NOBLE SPIRIT WILL OUTLIVE THE STARS.
I FEAR WE WILL ONLY EVER BE GUESTS HERE.
THE WORLD WILL ALWAYS *CHANGE* WHILE WE STAY THE *SAME*.

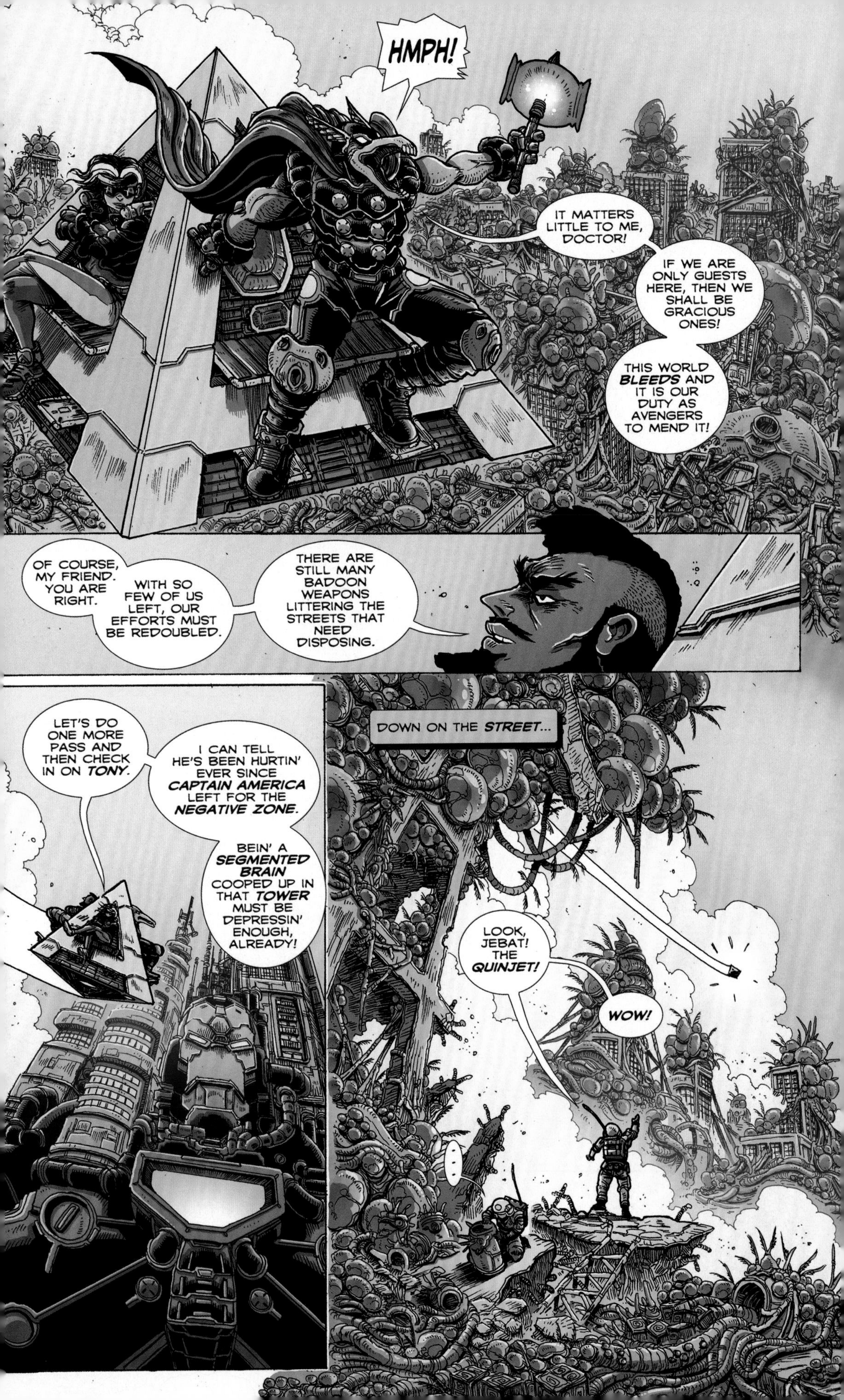
HMPH!
IT MATTERS LITTLE TO ME, DOCTOR!
IF WE ARE ONLY GUESTS HERE, THEN WE SHALL BE GRACIOUS ONES!
THIS WORLD BLEEDS AND IT IS OUR DUTY AS AVENGERS TO MEND IT!
OF COURSE, MY FRIEND. YOU ARE RIGHT.
WITH SO FEW OF US LEFT, OUR EFFORTS MUST BE REDOUBLED.
THERE ARE STILL MANY BADOON WEAPONS LITTERING THE STREETS THAT NEED DISPOSING.
LET'S DO ONE MORE PASS AND THEN CHECK IN ON TONY.
I CAN TELL HE'S BEEN HURTIN' EVER SINCE CAPTAIN AMERICA LEFT FOR THE NEGATIVE ZONE.
BEIN' A SEGMENTED BRAIN COOPED UP IN THAT TOWER MUST BE DEPRESSIN' ENOUGH, ALREADY!
DOWN ON THE STREET...
LOOK, JEBAT! THE QUINJET!
WOW!
...

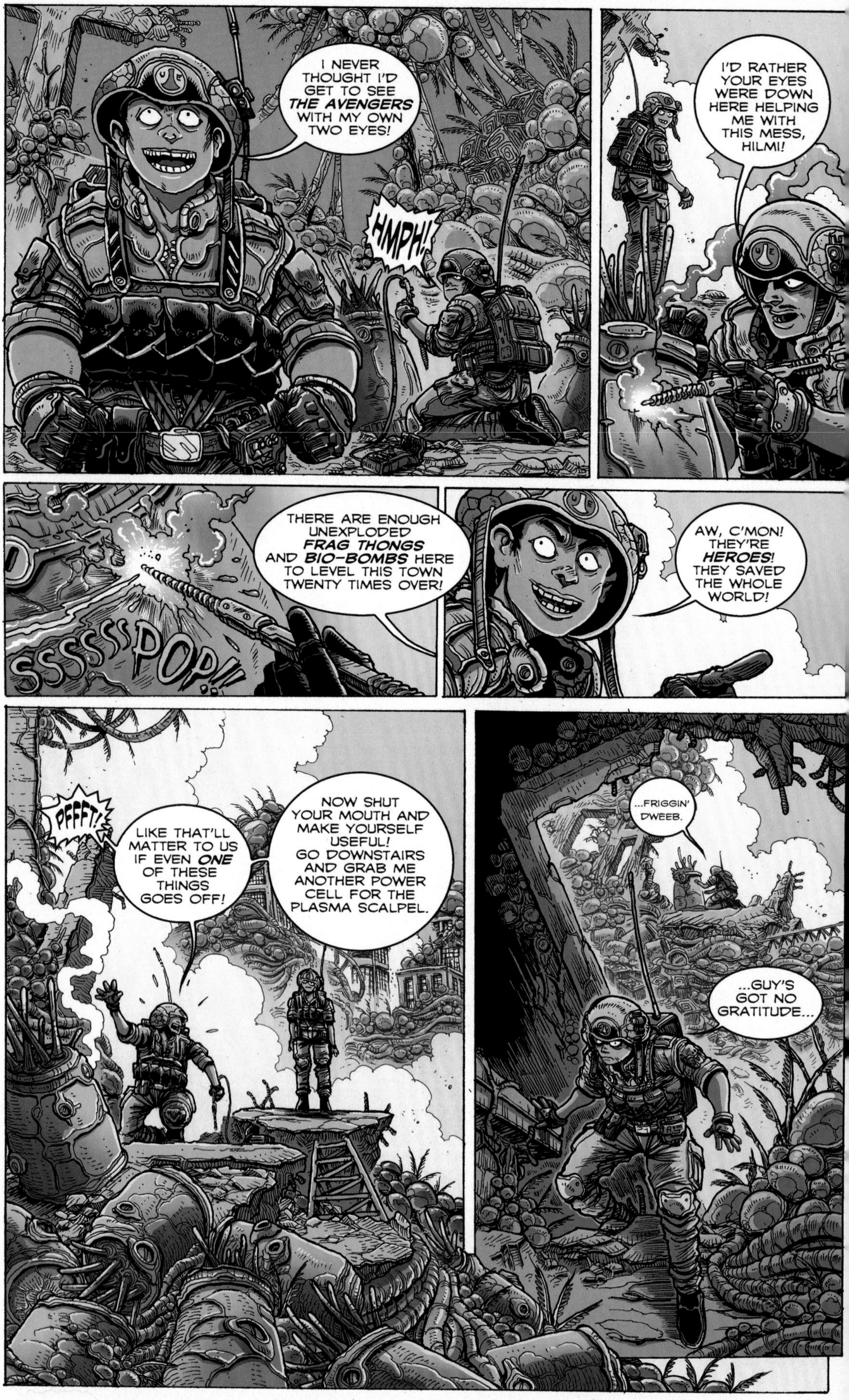
I NEVER THOUGHT I'D GET TO SEE THE AVENGERS WITH MY OWN TWO EYES!
HMPH!
I'D RATHER YOUR EYES WERE DOWN HERE HELPING ME WITH THIS MESS, HILMI!
THERE ARE ENOUGH UNEXPLODED FRAG THONGS AND BIO-BOMBS HERE TO LEVEL THIS TOWN TWENTY TIMES OVER!
SSSSSSPOP!!!
AW, C'MON! THEY'RE HEROES! THEY SAVED THE WHOLE WORLD!
PFFFT!
LIKE THAT'LL MATTER TO US IF EVEN ONE OF THESE THINGS GOES OFF!
NOW SHUT YOUR MOUTH AND MAKE YOURSELF USEFUL! GO DOWNSTAIRS AND GRAB ME ANOTHER POWER CELL FOR THE PLASMA SCALPEL.
...FRIGGIN' DWEEB.
...GUY'S GOT NO GRATITUDE...

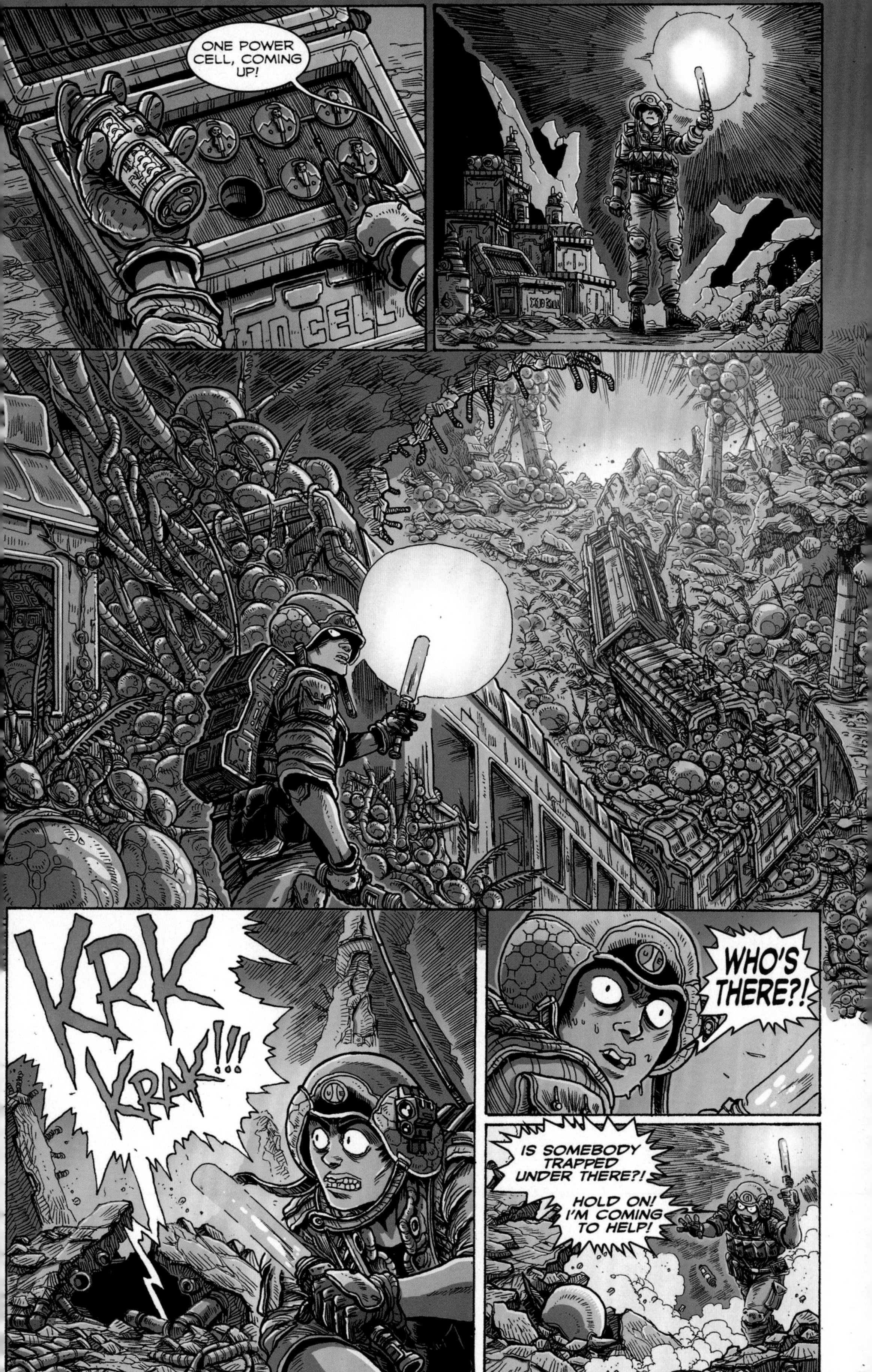
ONE POWER CELL, COMING UP!
10 CELL
KRK KRAK!!!
WHO'S THERE?!
IS SOMEBODY TRAPPED UNDER THERE?!
HOLD ON! I'M COMING TO HELP!

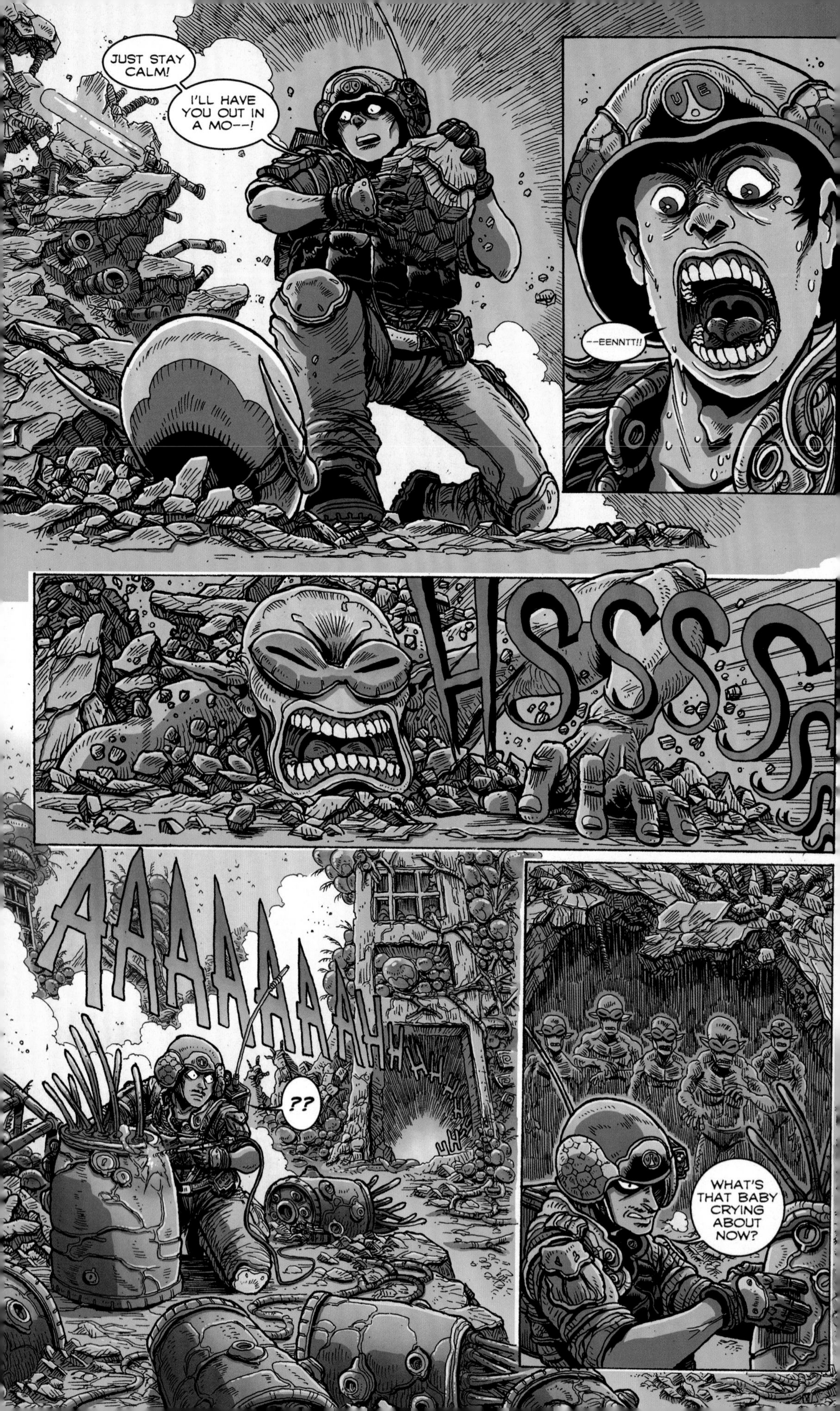
JUST STAY CALM!
I'LL HAVE YOU OUT IN A MO--!
--EENNTT!!
HSSSSS
AAAAAAAHH
??
WHAT'S THAT BABY CRYING ABOUT NOW?

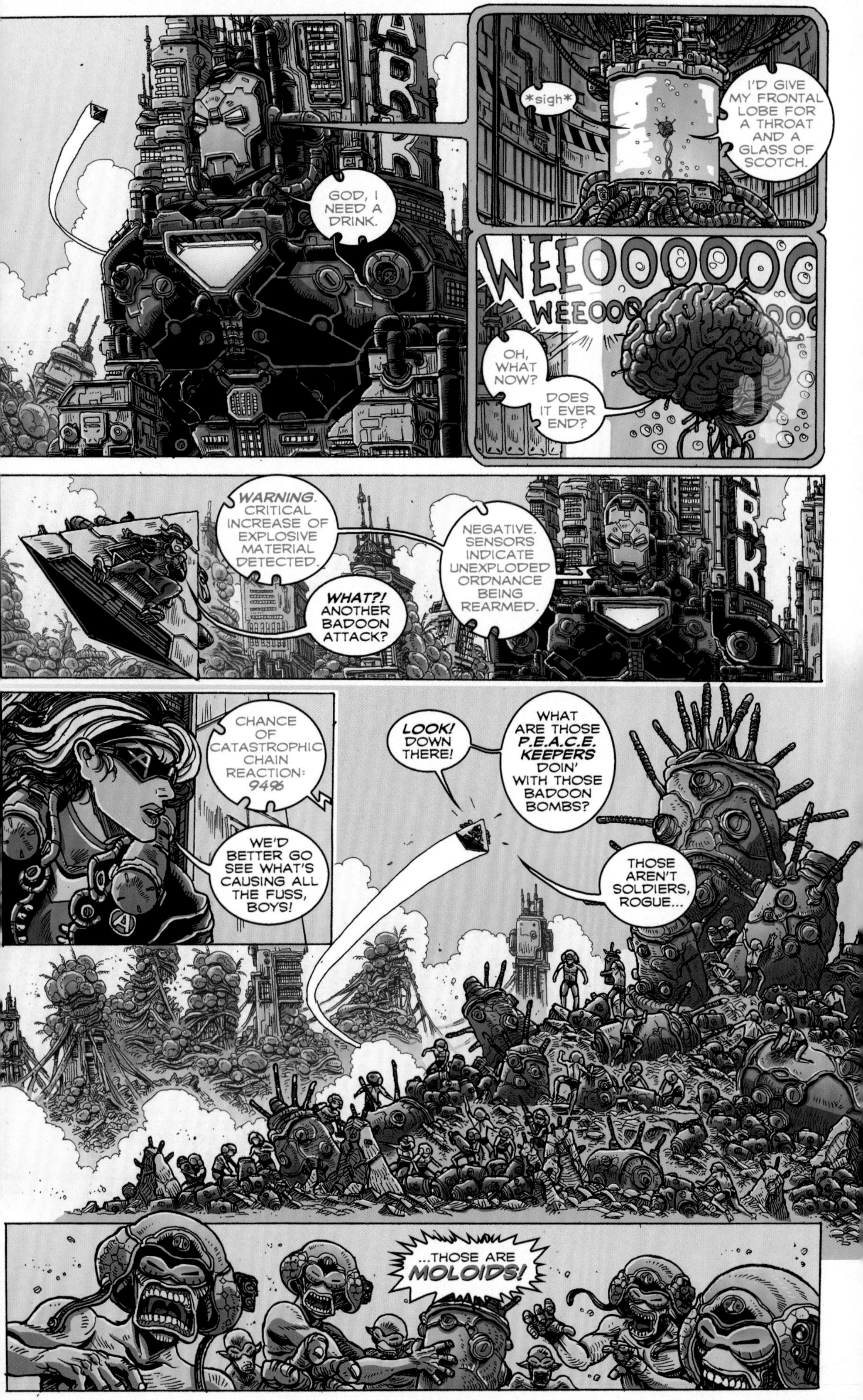
GOD, I NEED A DRINK.
sigh
I'D GIVE MY FRONTAL LOBE FOR A THROAT AND A GLASS OF SCOTCH.
WEEOOOOOO
WEEOOO
OH, WHAT NOW?
DOES IT EVER END?
WARNING. CRITICAL INCREASE OF EXPLOSIVE MATERIAL DETECTED.
WHAT?! ANOTHER BADOON ATTACK?
NEGATIVE. SENSORS INDICATE UNEXPLODED ORDNANCE BEING REARMED.
CHANCE OF CATASTROPHIC CHAIN REACTION: 94%
WE'D BETTER GO SEE WHAT'S CAUSING ALL THE FUSS, BOYS!
LOOK! DOWN THERE!
WHAT ARE THOSE P.E.A.C.E. KEEPERS DOIN' WITH THOSE BADOON BOMBS?
THOSE AREN'T SOLDIERS, ROGUE...
...THOSE ARE MOLOIDS!

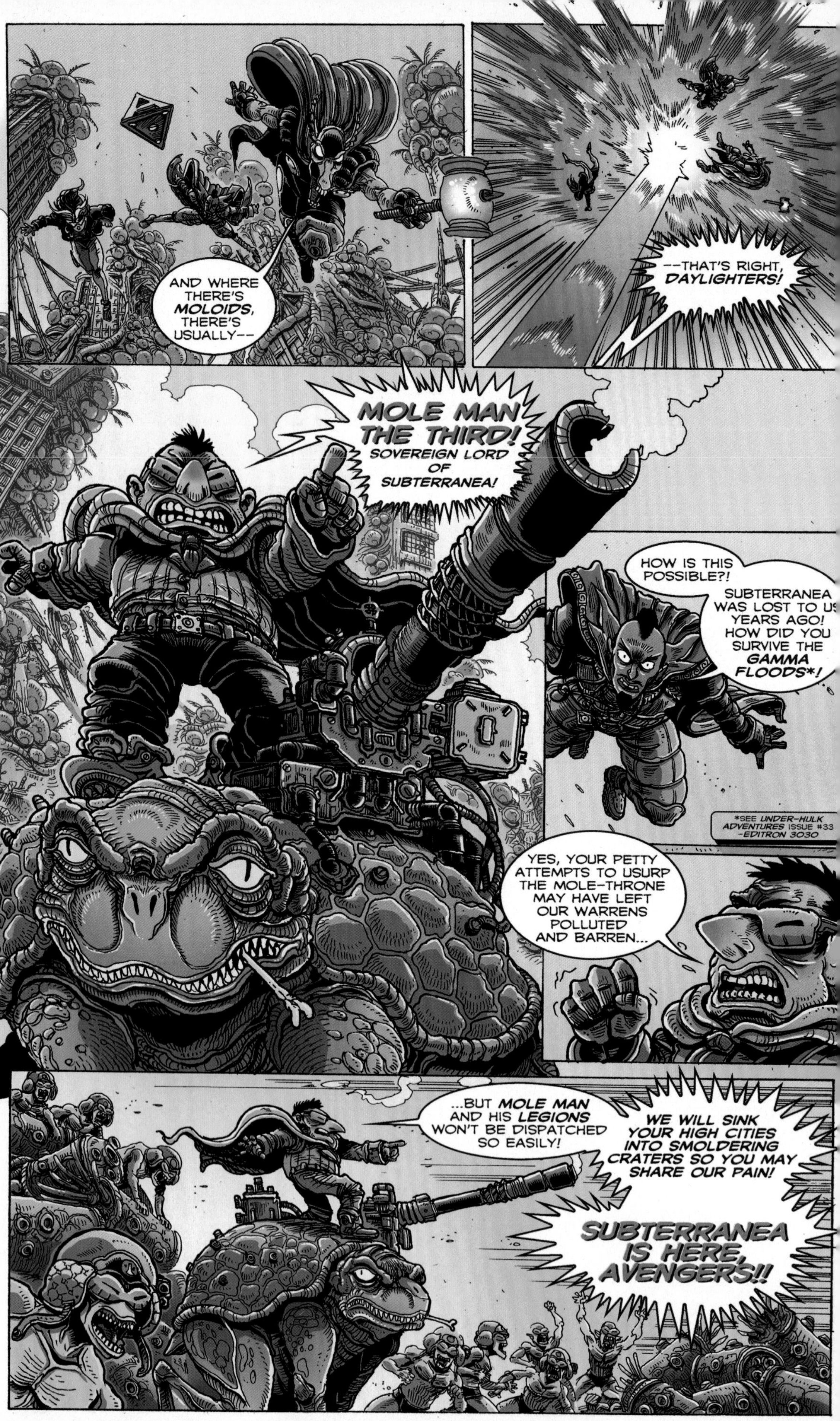

AND WHERE THERE'S MOLOIDS, THERE'S USUALLY--
--THAT'S RIGHT, DAYLIGHTERS!
MOLE MAN THE THIRD! SOVEREIGN LORD OF SUBTERRANEA!
HOW IS THIS POSSIBLE?!
SUBTERRANEA WAS LOST TO US YEARS AGO! HOW DID YOU SURVIVE THE GAMMA FLOODS*!
*SEE UNDER-HULK ADVENTURES ISSUE #33 -EDITRON 3030
YES, YOUR PETTY ATTEMPTS TO USURP THE MOLE-THRONE MAY HAVE LEFT OUR WARRENS POLLUTED AND BARREN...
...BUT MOLE MAN AND HIS LEGIONS WON'T BE DISPATCHED SO EASILY!
WE WILL SINK YOUR HIGH CITIES INTO SMOLDERING CRATERS SO YOU MAY SHARE OUR PAIN!
SUBTERRANEA IS HERE, AVENGERS!!

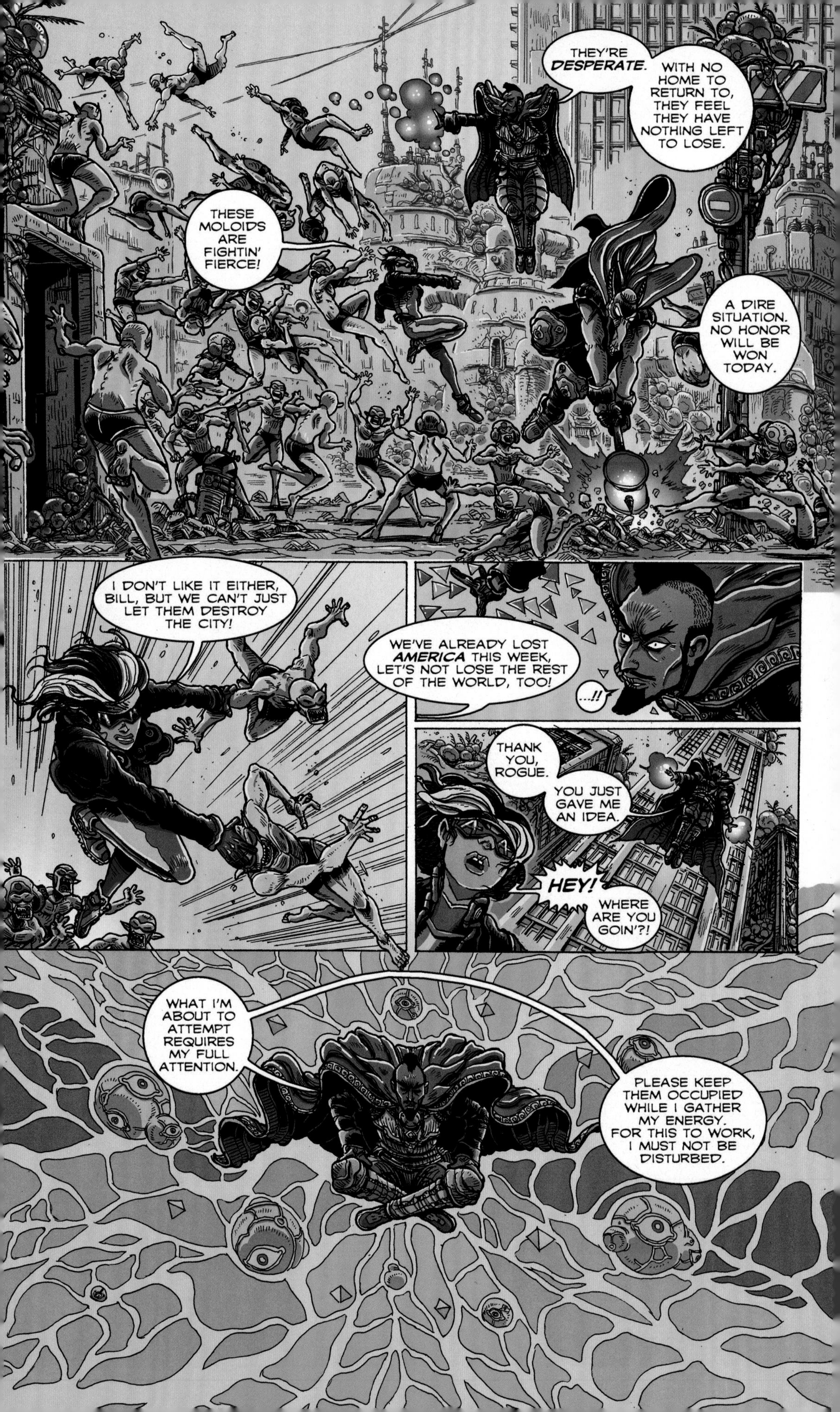
THEY'RE *DESPERATE*.
WITH NO HOME TO RETURN TO, THEY FEEL THEY HAVE NOTHING LEFT TO LOSE.
THESE MOLOIDS ARE FIGHTIN' FIERCE!
A DIRE SITUATION. NO HONOR WILL BE WON TODAY.
I DON'T LIKE IT EITHER, BILL, BUT WE CAN'T JUST LET THEM DESTROY THE CITY!
WE'VE ALREADY LOST *AMERICA* THIS WEEK, LET'S NOT LOSE THE REST OF THE WORLD, TOO!
...!!
THANK YOU, ROGUE.
YOU JUST GAVE ME AN IDEA.
HEY!
WHERE ARE YOU GOIN'?!
WHAT I'M ABOUT TO ATTEMPT REQUIRES MY FULL ATTENTION.
PLEASE KEEP THEM OCCUPIED WHILE I GATHER MY ENERGY. FOR THIS TO WORK, I MUST NOT BE DISTURBED.

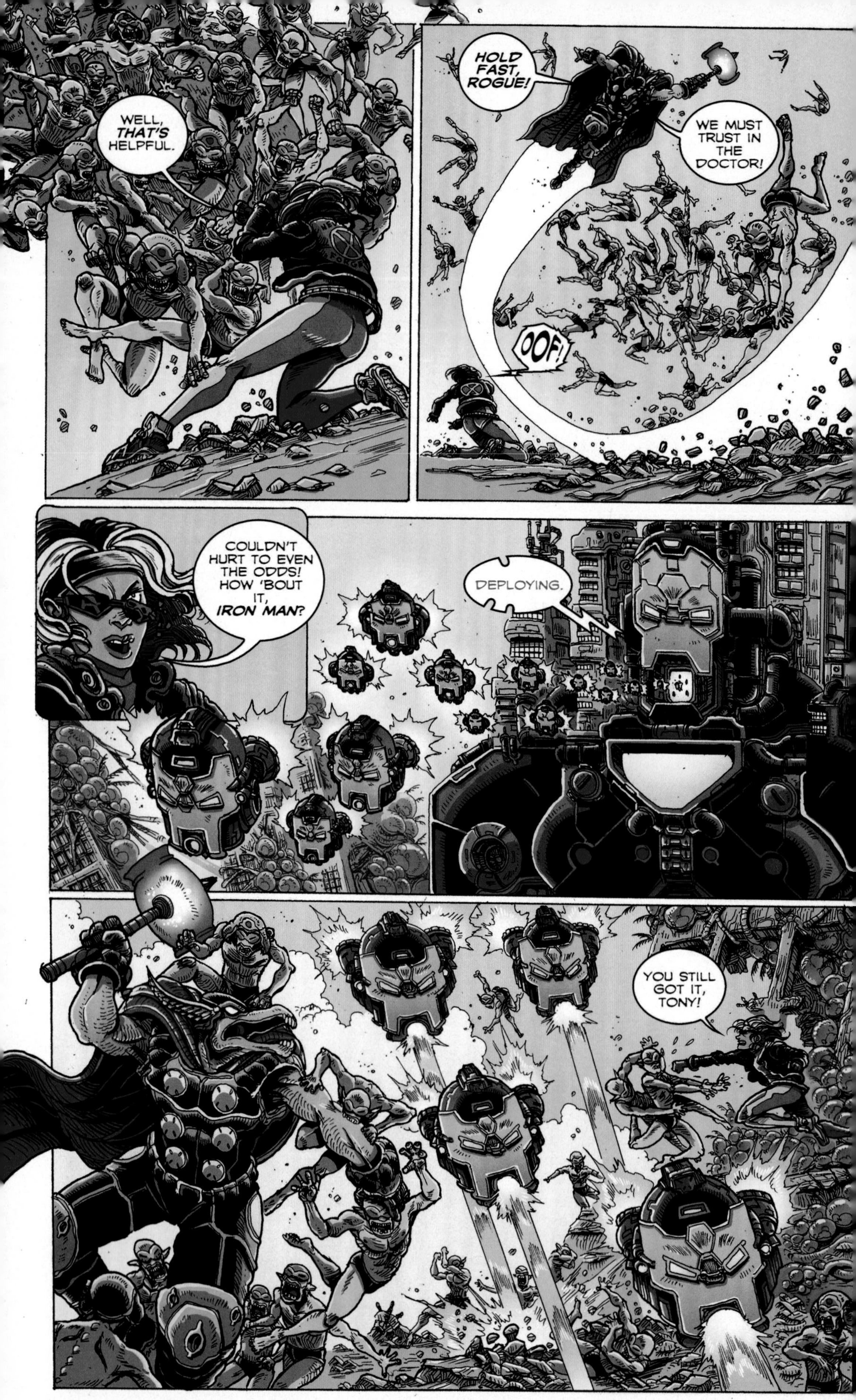
WELL, THAT'S HELPFUL.
HOLD FAST, ROGUE!
WE MUST TRUST IN THE DOCTOR!
OOF!
COULDN'T HURT TO EVEN THE ODDS! HOW 'BOUT IT, IRON MAN?
DEPLOYING.
YOU STILL GOT IT, TONY!

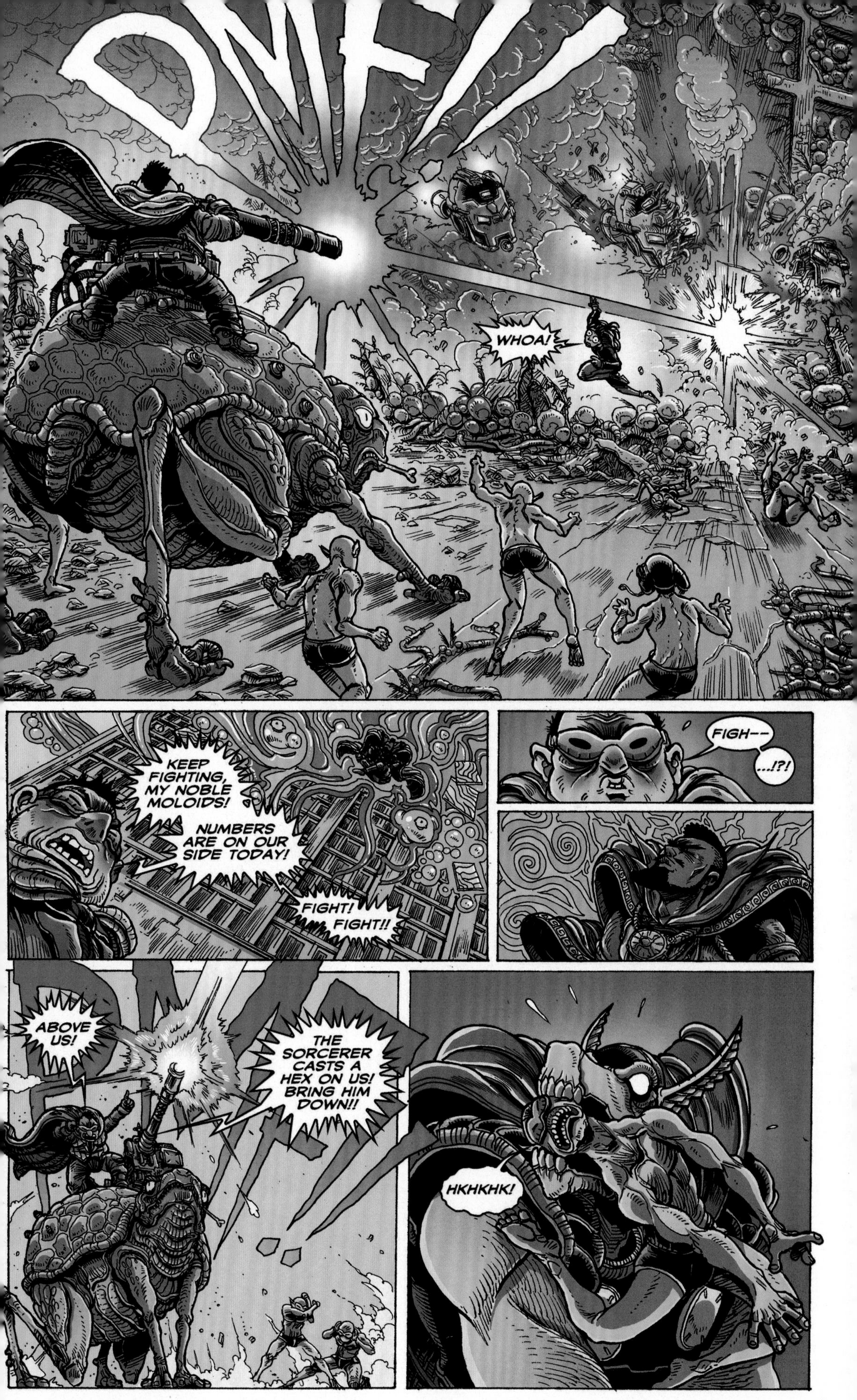
DMH!
WHOA!
KEEP FIGHTING, MY NOBLE MOLOIDS!
NUMBERS ARE ON OUR SIDE TODAY!
FIGHT! FIGHT!!
FIGH--
...!?!
ABOVE US!
THE SORCERER CASTS A HEX ON US! BRING HIM DOWN!!
HKHKHK!

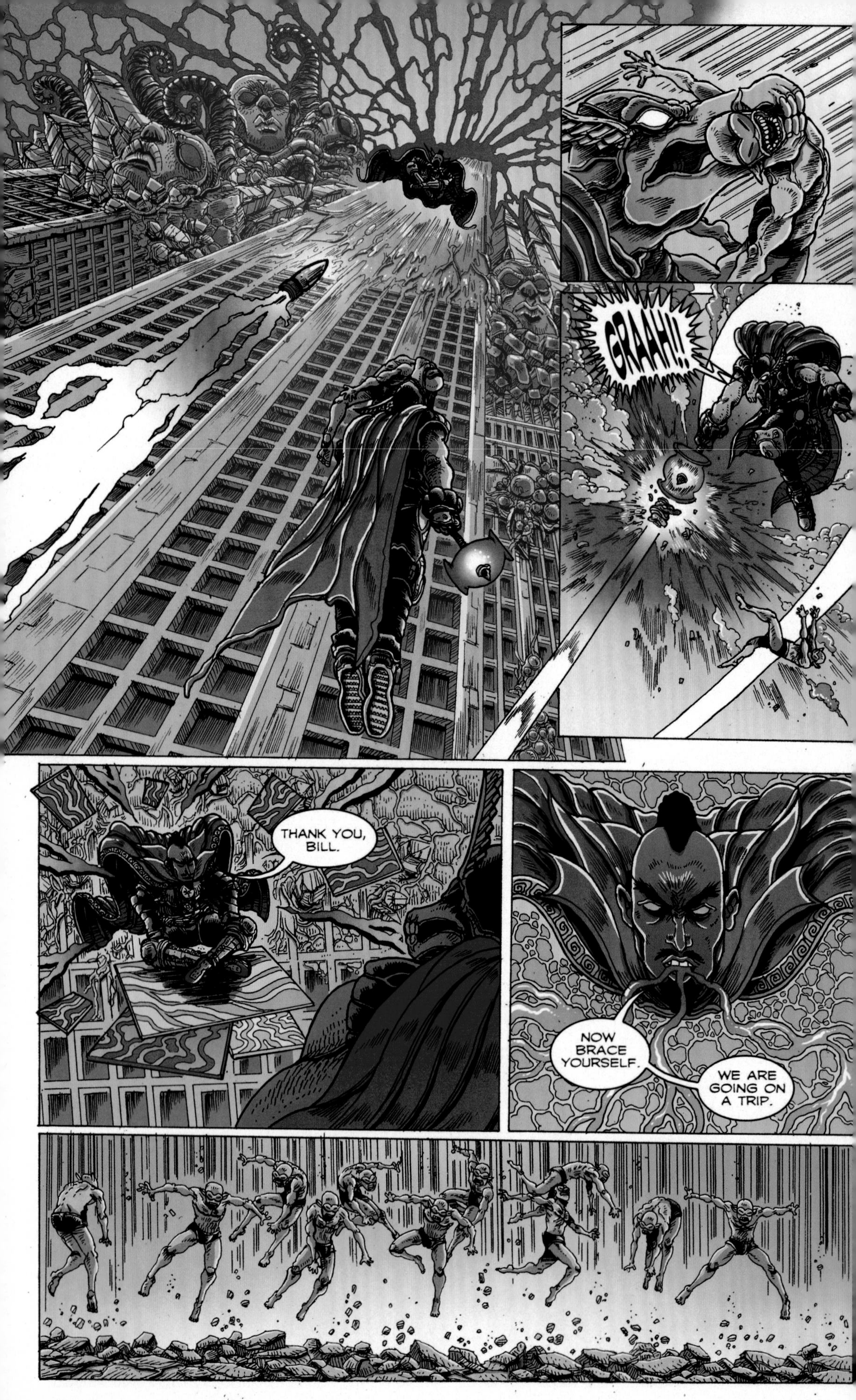
GRAAH!!
THANK YOU, BILL.
NOW BRACE YOURSELF.
WE ARE GOING ON A TRIP.

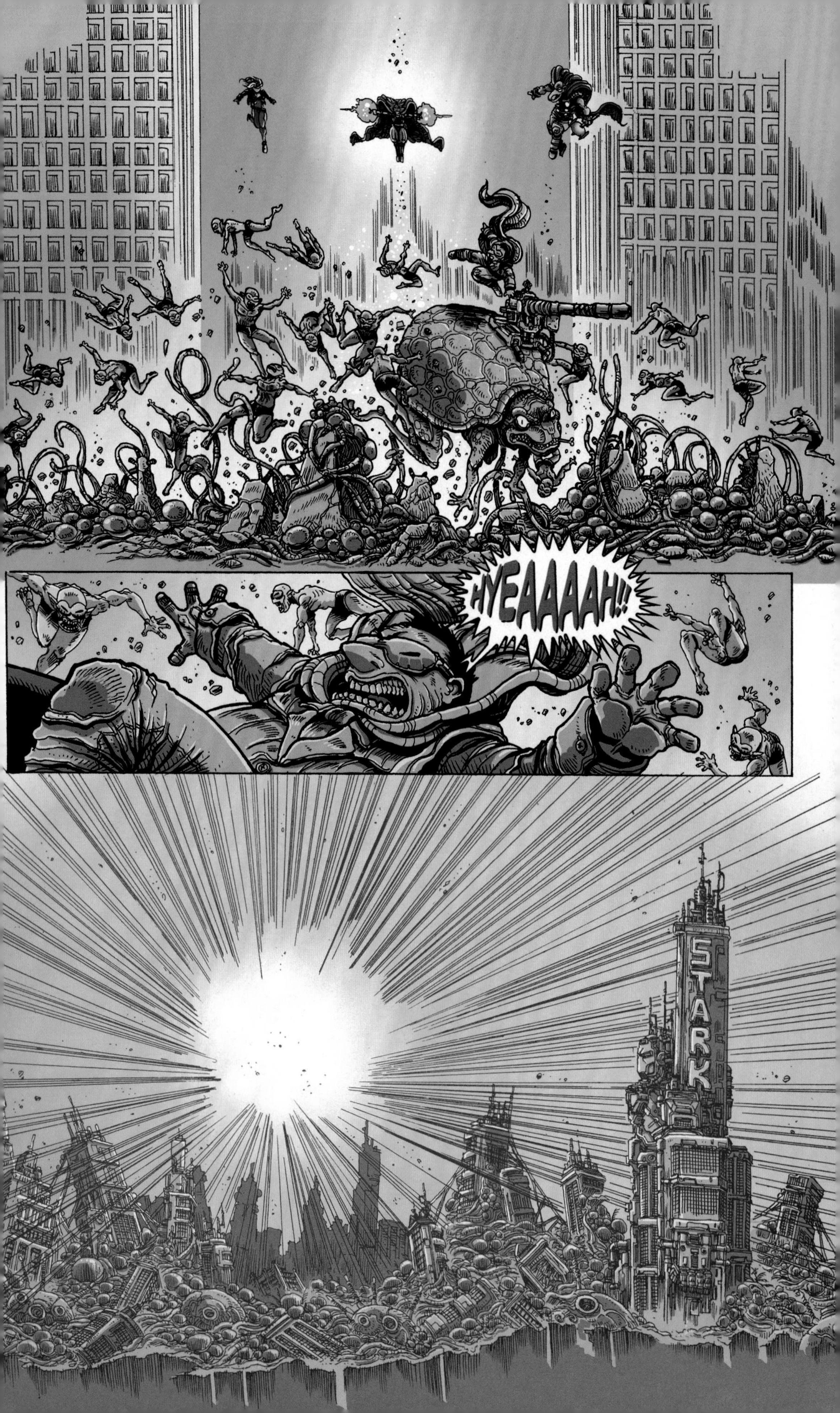
HYEAAAAH!!
STARK

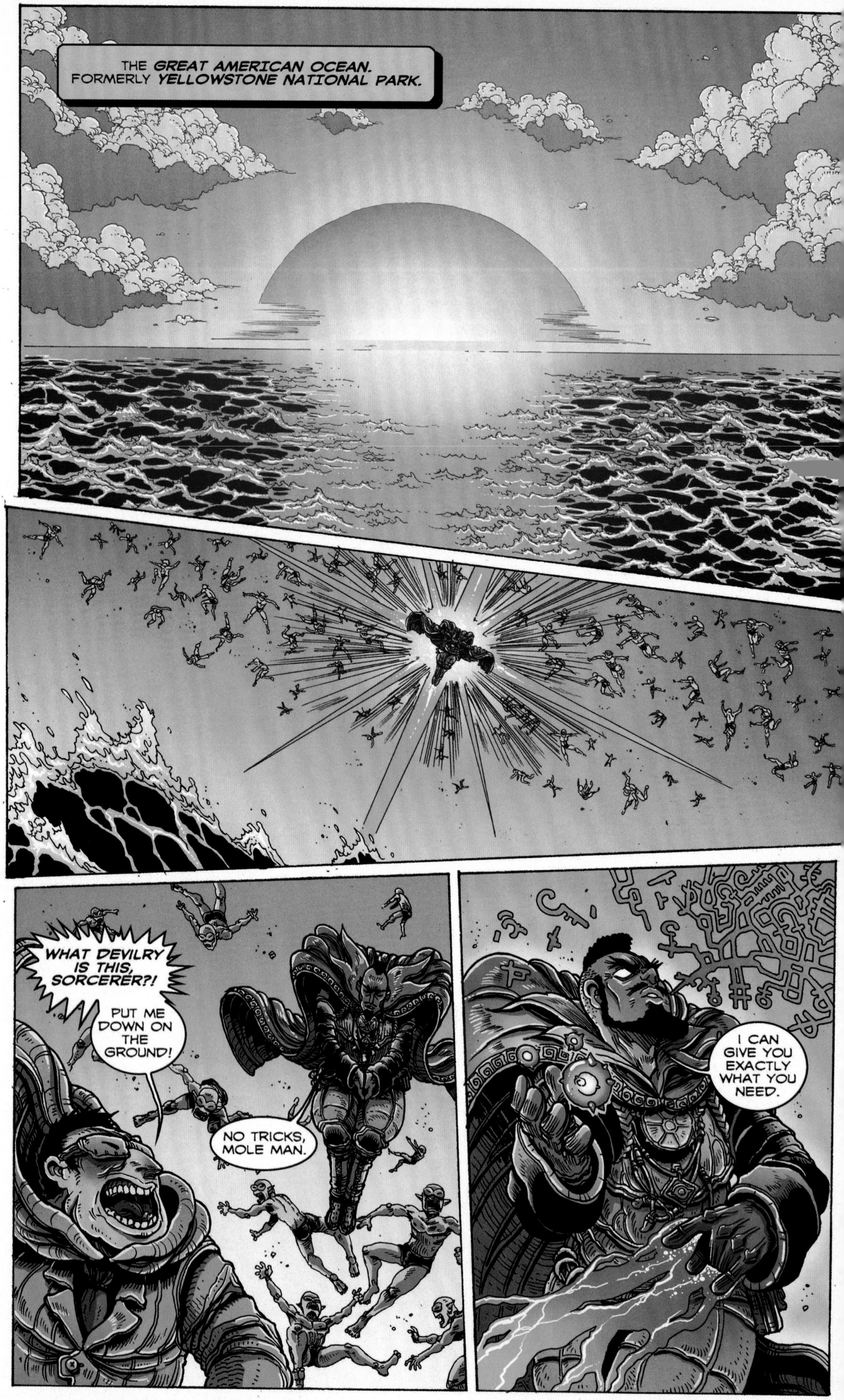
THE GREAT AMERICAN OCEAN.
FORMERLY YELLOWSTONE NATIONAL PARK.
WHAT DEVILRY IS THIS, SORCERER?!
PUT ME DOWN ON THE GROUND!
NO TRICKS, MOLE MAN.
I CAN GIVE YOU EXACTLY WHAT YOU NEED.

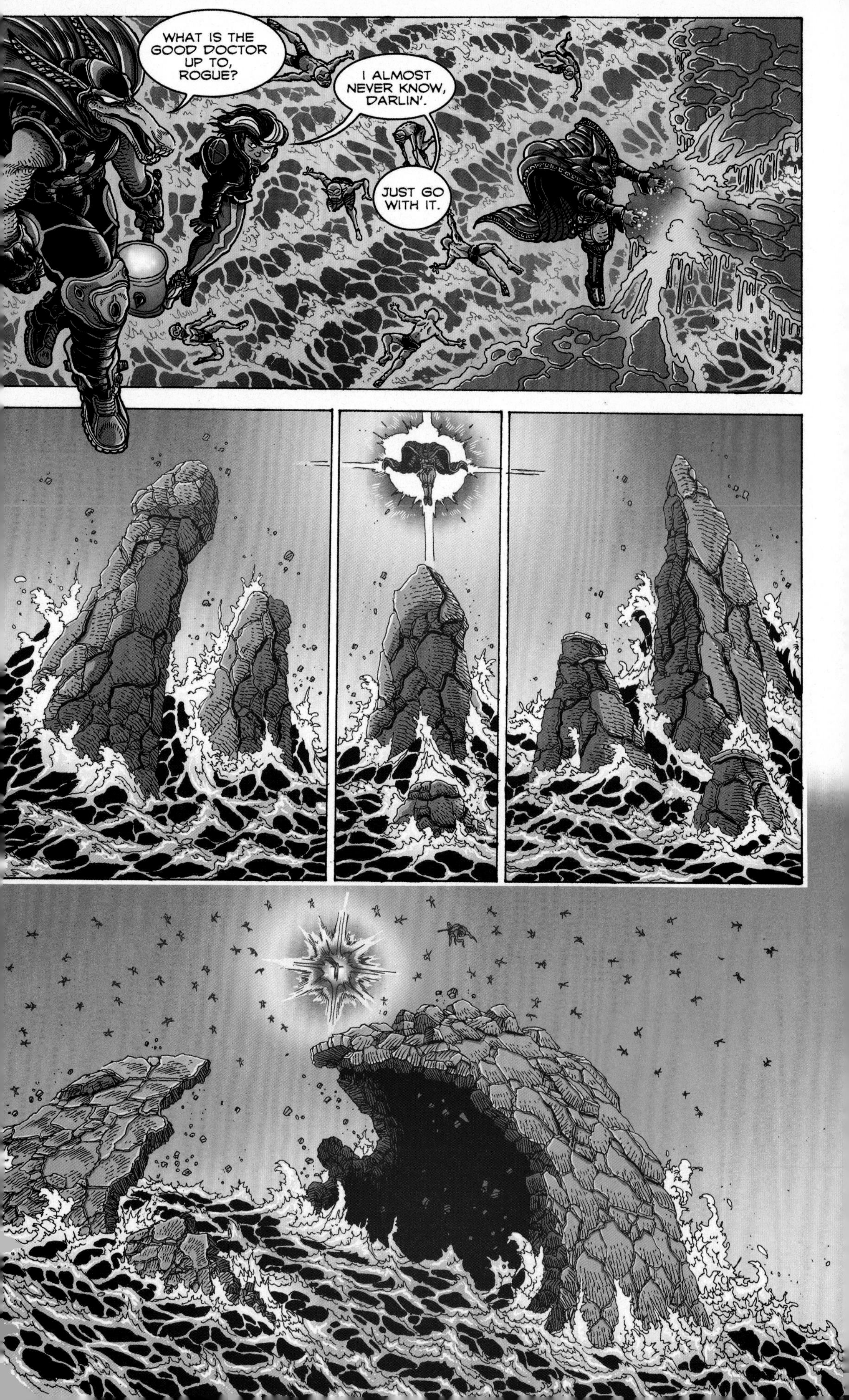
WHAT IS THE GOOD DOCTOR UP TO, ROGUE?
I ALMOST NEVER KNOW, DARLIN'.
JUST GO WITH IT.

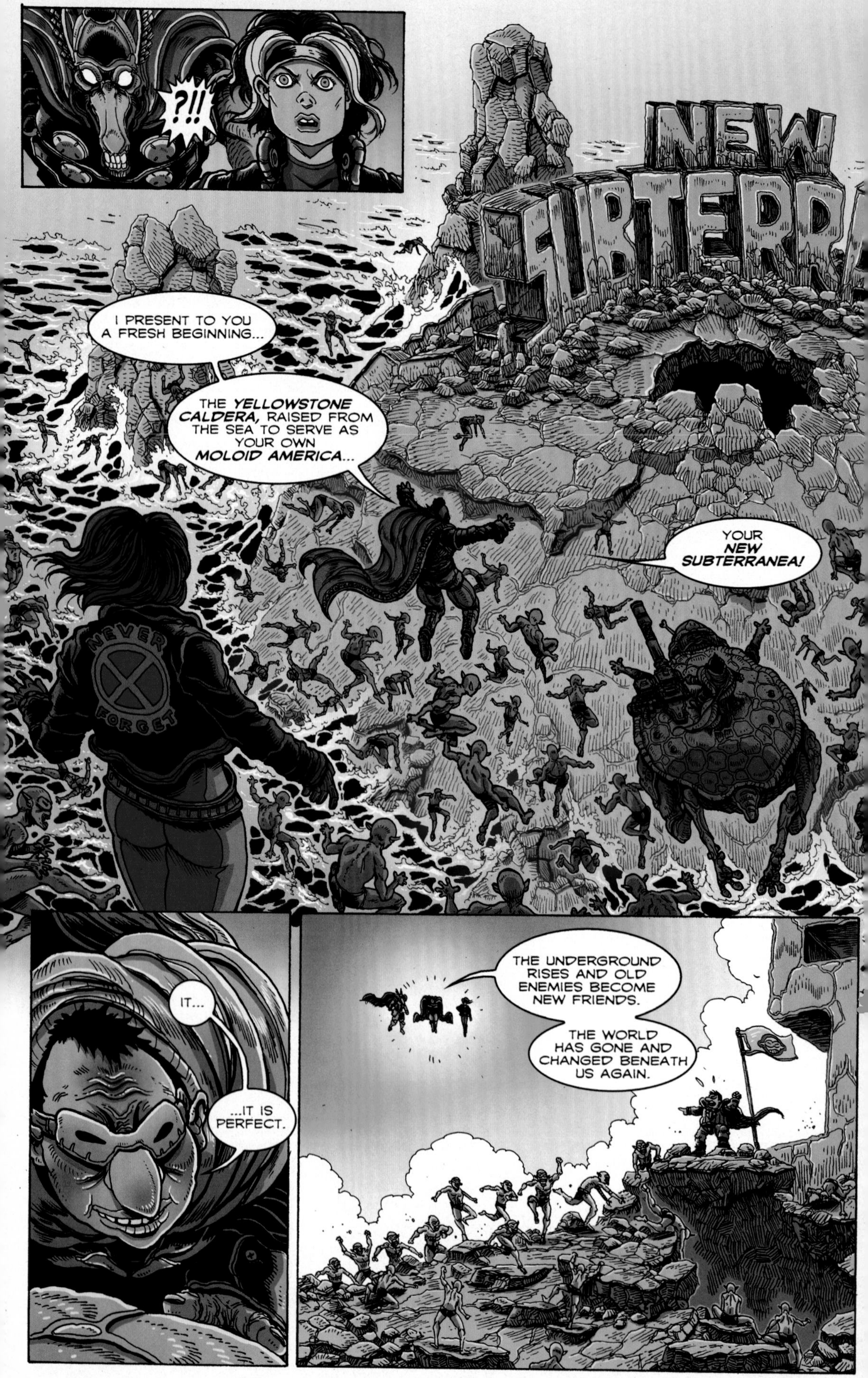
?!!
NEW SUBTERRA
I PRESENT TO YOU A FRESH BEGINNING...
THE YELLOWSTONE CALDERA, RAISED FROM THE SEA TO SERVE AS YOUR OWN MOLOID AMERICA...
YOUR NEW SUBTERRANEA!
NEVER FORGET
IT...
...IT IS PERFECT.
THE UNDERGROUND RISES AND OLD ENEMIES BECOME NEW FRIENDS.
THE WORLD HAS GONE AND CHANGED BENEATH US AGAIN.

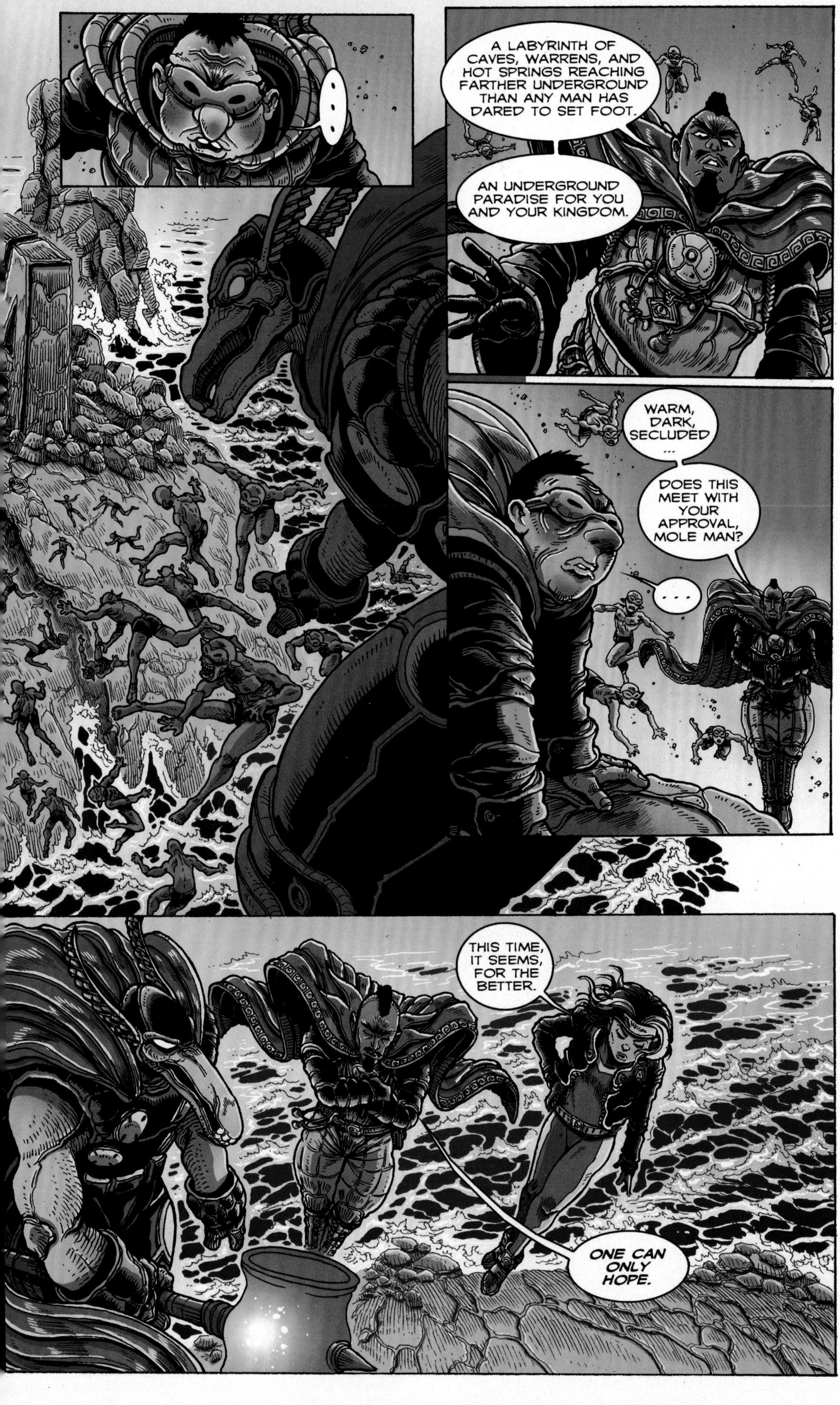
. . .
A LABYRINTH OF CAVES, WARRENS, AND HOT SPRINGS REACHING FARTHER UNDERGROUND THAN ANY MAN HAS DARED TO SET FOOT.
AN UNDERGROUND PARADISE FOR YOU AND YOUR KINGDOM.
WARM, DARK, SECLUDED ...
DOES THIS MEET WITH YOUR APPROVAL, MOLE MAN?
. . .
THIS TIME, IT SEEMS, FOR THE BETTER.
ONE CAN ONLY HOPE.

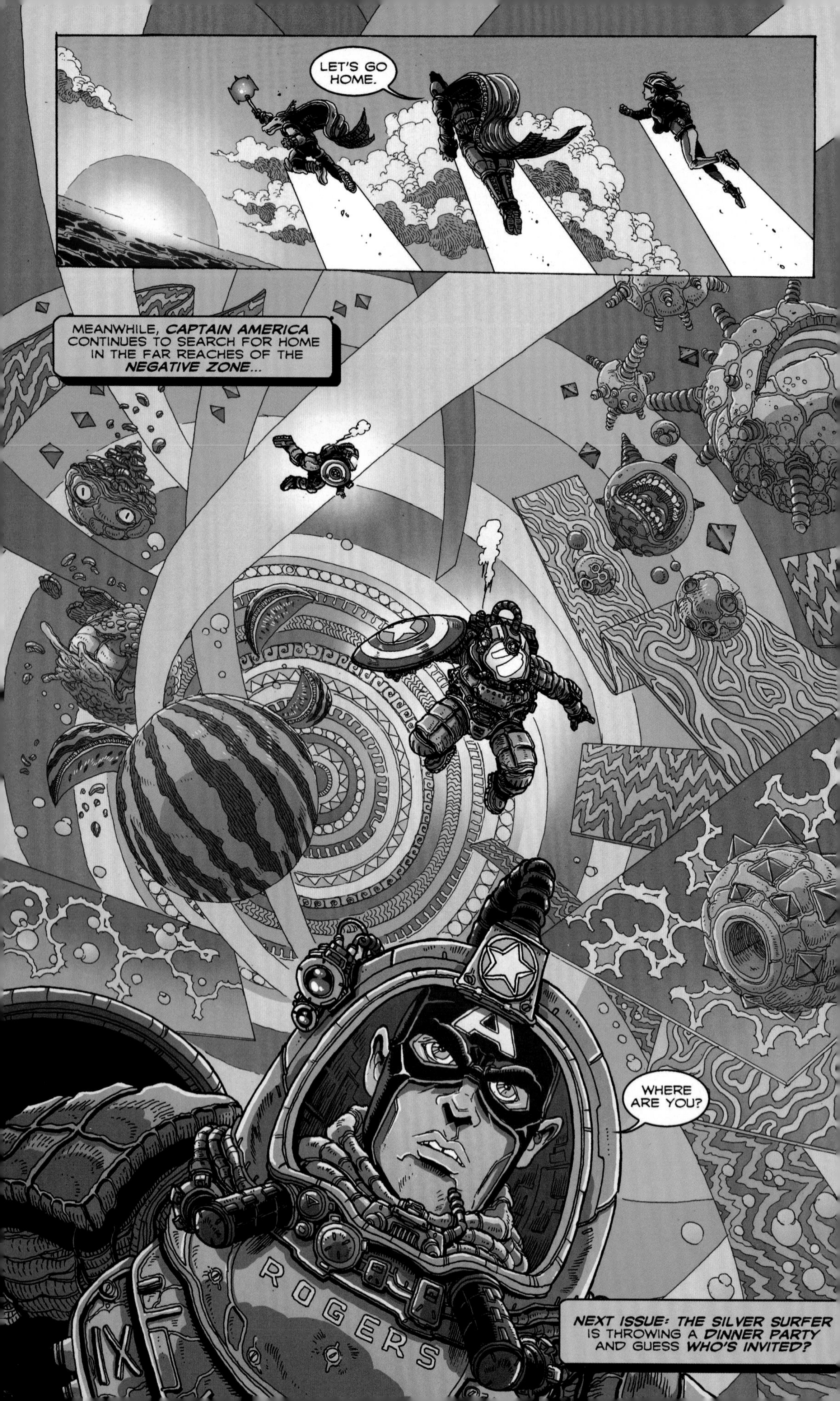
LET'S GO HOME.
MEANWHILE, CAPTAIN AMERICA CONTINUES TO SEARCH FOR HOME IN THE FAR REACHES OF THE NEGATIVE ZONE...
WHERE ARE YOU?
ROGERS
NEXT ISSUE: THE SILVER SURFER IS THROWING A DINNER PARTY AND GUESS WHO'S INVITED?

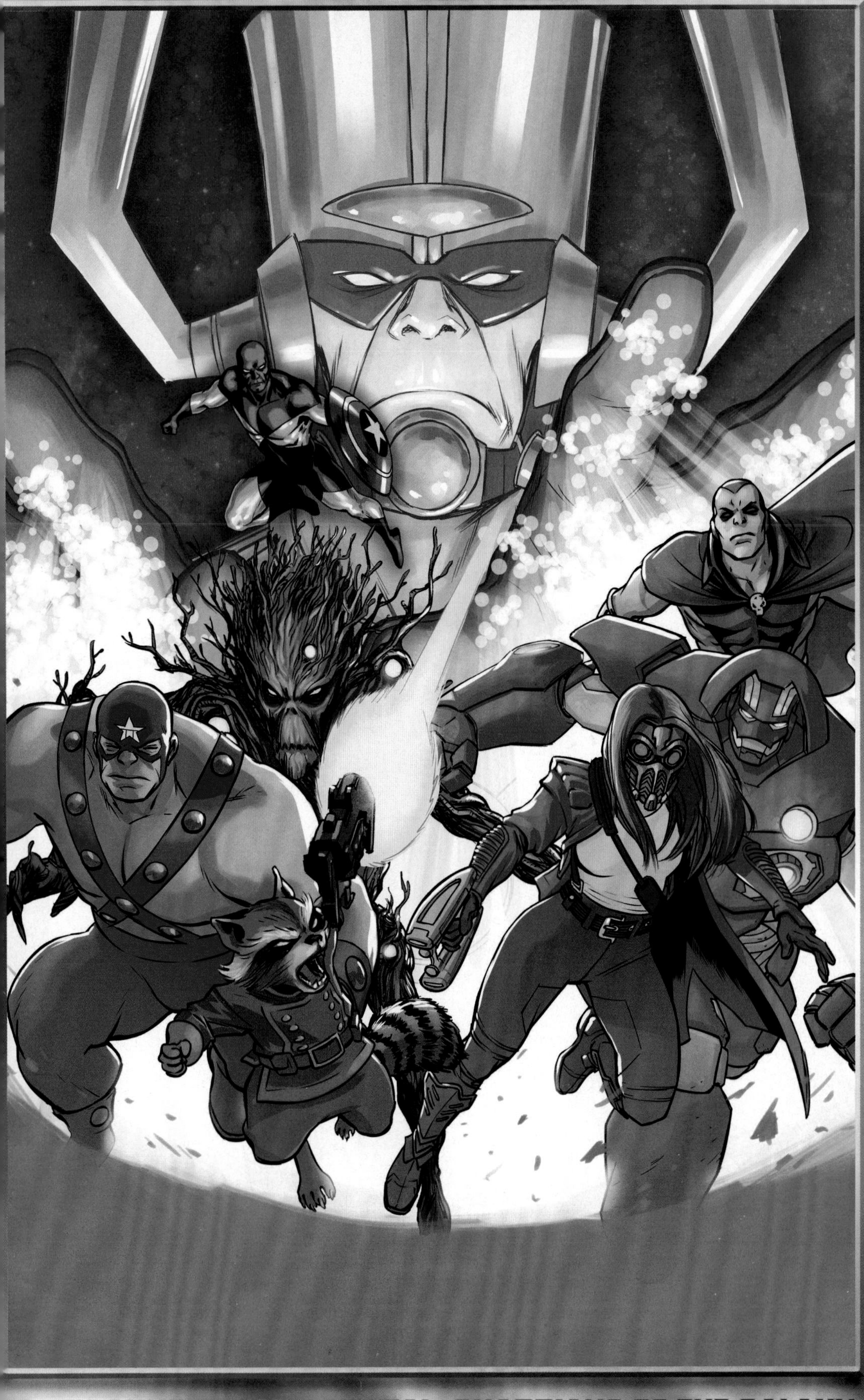

100TH ANNIVERSARY SPECIAL: GUARDIANS OF THE GALAXY

GUARDIANS OF THE GALAXY

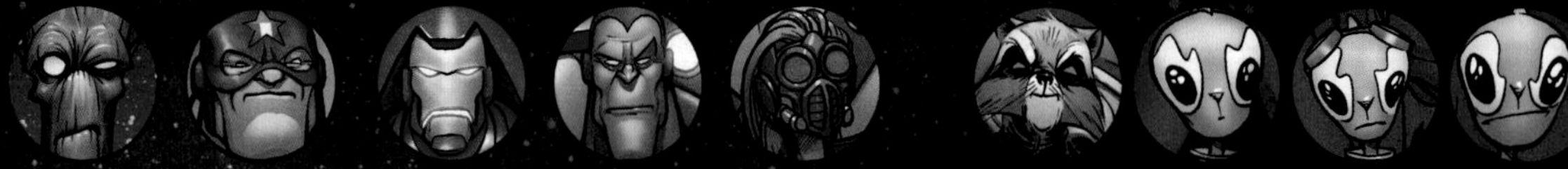

GROOT   CHARLIE-27   IRON MAN   DRAX   STAR-LORD   ROCKET AND THE RACCOONS

THE LIVING TRIBUNAL GRANTED THE SILVER SURFER A SINGLE MOMENT OF GODHOOD, BESTOWING THE COSMIC HERO WITH A GLIMPSE OF OMNIPOTENCE. CRAVING SUCH POWER, GALACTUS REABSORBED THE SILVER SURFER, BECOMING SILVER GALACTUS, A BEING WITH A GREATER HUNGER THAN EVER BEFORE.

NOW, IN THE WAKE OF THE ANNIHILATION APOCALYPSE THE UNIVERSE HAS BECOME A DANGEROUS AND UNSTABLE PLACE. THE FABRIC OF SPACE AND TIME HAS BEEN TWISTED AND TORN, COSMIC EMPIRES PREPARE FOR WAR AND INTERGALACTIC TERRORISTS THREATEN WHATEVER PEACE EXISTS.

IN THESE CHAOTIC AND DESPERATE TIMES, ONE TEAM STANDS BETWEEN THE UNIVERSE AND OBLIVION. ONE TEAM FIGHTS FOR THE HELPLESS AND PROTECTS THE VULNERABLE. ONE TEAM MADE UP OF AN ASSASSIN, A MANIAC, A CLONE, A CYBORG, A TREE AND SOME RACCOONS. TOGETHER THEY ARE COSMIC CHAMPIONS, THE GUARDIANS OF THE GALAXY!

ANDY LANNING AND RON MARZ
WRITERS

GUSTAVO DUARTE
ARTIST

EDGAR DELGADO
COLOR ARTIST

DAVID LOPEZ
COVER ARTIST

ALEXANDER LOZANO
VARIANT ARTIST

VC's JOE SABINO
LETTERER

DEVIN LEWIS
EDITOR

NICK LOWE
SENIOR EDITOR

AXEL ALONSO
EDITOR IN CHIEF

JOE QUESADA
CHIEF CREATIVE OFFICER

DAN BUCKLEY
PUBLISHER

ALAN FINE
EXECUTIVE PRODUCER